If God Has a Plan For My Life,

You
Have a
Destiny

Why Can't I Find It??

If God Has a Plan For My Life,

You Have a Destiny

Why Can't I Find It??

RON BOEHME

YWAM Publishing
A Ministry of Youth With A Mission
P.O. Box 55787, Seattle, WA 98155

If God Has a Plan for My Life, Why Can't I Find It?

Copyright © 1992 by Ron Boehme

Published by Youth With A Mission Publishing,
P.O. Box 55787, Seattle, WA 98155, USA.

Unless noted otherwise, all Scripture quotations are taken from The Holy Bible, New Century Version, copyright 1987, 1988, 1991 by Word Publishing, Dallas, Texas 75039. Used by permission.

ISBN 0-927545-42-X

Printed in the United States of America

To our children,

Nathan, son of promise,
David and Bethany, twin confirmations of blessing,
Megan, our sweet singer,
and Ryan, who wouldn't have been born
if we didn't believe that
God had another eternal destiny
to bring into this world.

May each of you fulfill
your God-given destinies.

Acknowledgments

John Wesley was once asked how long it took to write a sermon. "Twenty-five years," he replied. "Because it takes 25 years to make a man."

If the same is true of books, it took 39 years for me to write this book, and I am deeply indebted to all the people who encouraged me along the way.

Loren Cunningham and the men and women of destiny who serve in Youth With A Mission have been my main mentors. That's why it's been easy to give almost 20 years of my life to working alongside them in the task of world evangelism. Their knowledge and pursuit of God's call have been a steady inspiration.

Special thanks are given to Shirley Sells, my editor, and Jim and Janice Rogers, Pam Warren, Tom and Terry Bragg, and Warren Walsh with YWAM Publishing. Your encouragement and help have made this project a smooth one. Because you've been faithful to fulfill your own destiny through literature, I'm able to offer this particular contribution.

Table of Contents

Foreword

You were born into a world of unprecedented change. For the first time ever in the history of mankind, the wilderness is safer than civilization. Old nations vanish overnight; new nations are born in a day. As Casey Stengel said, "The future ain't what it used to be." Never in the history of the West have we had a greater need for men and women of God with a sure sense of His call on their lives, and a consciousness of the significance of the times in which they live.

"You are a chosen generation, a royal priesthood, a holy nation." The day you gave your life to Jesus Christ, you began a great and wonderful adventure into the future. It is the heritage of every true child of God. Saints of old knew it as being part of the Chosen People. It gave them courage when times got tough. It made them strong in the face of trial. It gave them vision when they could hardly see, because they already had a glimpse of their future in God. They knew they were special, because the King of Kings had made them not only children of His royal family, but ambassadors in His army, and messengers of His mission. They felt clean and chosen and commissioned. It was a sense of divine destiny.

Now this book will not give you what they had. No book but *the book of your own life, written under His direction,* has that material. And only the Living God can write that for you as you set your heart on seeking Him, and meet with Him in the still and secret places that only He will see. But all of us learn things in life that can help open the door for God to speak to us and keep us faithful to that special calling He has for us.

This is the personal and practical advice of a man who has seen God's dealings in his own life. In this book, Ron will help you discover things that will help clear the way for you to be the kind of man or woman Christ died for you to be.

"It is time to prepare ourselves for an unprecedented revival," says Gary North. It is time to prepare ourselves for the changing of the guard in every area of life all over the world. Our preparation must help us answer the question: *"I'm saved; what now?"*

And now it is your turn. Our poor, broken world needs people who will pay the price to affect homes, streets, cities, and even nations in every level of society. Take this simple journey with Ron Boehme as part of that crucial preparation. This is your day to find your place in history. And *"who knows whether you have come into the Kingdom for such a time as this?"*

—Winkie Pratney

Section I

You Have a Destiny—Believe It

You made my whole being; you formed me in my mother's body. I praise you because you made me in an amazing and wonderful way. What you have done is wonderful. I know this very well. You saw my bones being formed as I took shape in my mother's body. When I was put together there, you saw my body as it was formed. All the days planned for me were written in your book before I was one day old (Psalm 139:13-16).

God made each of us for a specific purpose. We are not biological accidents meant to wander aimlessly on this earth. Our unique characteristics, circumstances, and calling are part of a grand design and what make us special to Him.

In this section, we will attempt to see ourselves from God's viewpoint and expose one of the cruelest hoaxes of all time—a lie that has spiritually crippled millions of people.

God wants us to discover and live out His wonderful plan for our lives. The adventure begins when we *see* our personal destiny and *believe* that He will give us the grace and power to fulfill it.

1

Why in the World Am I Here?

I remember exactly when my life changed. It happened late one night in a very unlikely place.

"Why do you think God brought us into this world?" I asked a friend. We were in a popular fast-food restaurant where students went for a break. We'd just been making small talk when I blurted out the question. But it had weighed on my mind for months.

He didn't seem to have a clue. Like me, he'd gone away to college to "find himself." We were freshmen at a prestigious university in the Pacific Northwest. From having been an all-conference athlete and valedictorian of my senior class, I was at a point now where I couldn't even decide on a major.

He finally answered, "You know, Ron, maybe we should just get outta here and find out."

That's all I needed to hear. I almost fell off my chair in excitement. I already had something in mind, and was just waiting for confirmation. As if prompted by some inner voice, I raced ahead. "Let's go to New Zealand!" I said. "I spent a great summer there in 1970. We'll leave our distractions behind and really try to find out the Lord's will for our lives."

We began to plan. By the time we left the restaurant, we had worked out most of the details.

And so my adventure began.

I finished out the school year. In the fall of 1973,

I gave up a full-ride, athletic-academic scholarship to begin my search for God. Along with that friend and two others, I spent the next year traveling and studying in New Zealand. By the time I returned home, my perspective on life had changed.

I never went back to college.

It wasn't where I went that made any difference. Just that I'd taken a step of obedience in faith. In all the years since, God has continued to reveal to me His plan for my life. Sometimes He's made His wishes abundantly clear. Sometimes I've had to search hard for answers. There have been testings. There have been painful detours. Yet I have always known that the secret to a fulfilling life is in knowing God's plan for it.

First, He called me to serve Him full-time by directing me to become a missionary. He took me to Europe to be trained, focused, and launched.

A year later, God led me to the person who was to be my wife. Shirley Cookson and I were married October 10, 1976. Then God showed me the nation I was to call home, and the ministry we were to begin.

Recognizing and fulfilling my destiny has brought me tremendous joy. God wants that same joy for each person He creates. Let's explore together a promise that can change your life: *you, too, have a God-given destiny.*

D-Day for the Apostle Paul

The apostle Paul is one of my favorite examples of a man who discovered his destiny. He came from a good family. He was well educated. In all ways, he seemed to be "the guy most likely to succeed." But his early life was filled with hatred toward Christians, and the extent of his involvement in prison ministry was to put them in jail! It all changed one day when he met Jesus on the road to Damascus. In Acts 26:14-22, Jesus said to him:

"Saul, Saul, why are you persecuting me? You are only hurting yourself by fighting me." I said, "Who are you, Lord?" The Lord said, "I am Jesus, the one you are persecuting. Stand up! I have chosen you to be my servant and my witness—you will tell people the things that you have seen and the things that I will show you. This is why I have come to you today. I will keep you safe from your own people and also from those who are not Jewish. I am sending you to them to open their eyes so that they may turn away from darkness to the light, away from the power of Satan and to God. Then their sins can be forgiven, and they can have a place with those people who have been made holy by believing in me."

"King Agrippa, after I had this vision from heaven, I obeyed it...But God has helped me, and so I stand here today, telling all people, small and great, what I have seen."

On the day of Paul's conversion, *he was given his destiny in God.* Years of study and preparation lay ahead, dangers and difficulties. But Jesus told him that day why he had been created. To be a servant. To deliver a message to the non-Jewish world. Many years later, he would humbly and confidently tell King Agrippa that *he had obeyed the heavenly vision.*

You and I may not be a Paul. Most of us haven't killed Christians for a living, or been knocked to the ground by heavenly lights. (It took a lot to get Paul's attention!) But each of us has been given a destiny by our loving Creator.

God Has a Plan

During our visit to New Zealand in 1973, God gave me a wonderful lifetime verse that I regularly refer to. It's found in Jeremiah 29:11-14:

"I say this because I know what I am planning for you," says the Lord. "I have good plans for you, not plans to hurt you. I will give you hope and a good future. Then you will call my name. You will come to me and pray to me, and I will listen to you. You will search for me. And when you search for me with all your heart, you will find me! I will let you find me," says the Lord.

God promises us a good future. He says that He has plans for us. But He doesn't reveal Himself to the half-hearted seeker.

Years ago, I was having lunch with one of the most well-known Christian leaders in America. Toward the end of our conversation, he said to me, "Ron, I'm not fulfilled. I don't believe that I'm doing what God has called me to do."

I was stunned. This man had made a great impact on the world through his leadership and his writings. Yet he found himself in the same place that many others do. He was uncertain about his destiny. It brought home an important point to me: regardless of a person's age or place in life, it's never too late (nor too early) to seek God's will for your life.

How about You?

This book has been written to encourage you to *be the person you were created to be.*

The book is divided into major sections. The first focuses on what we must *believe*, the second on what we must *achieve*, and the third on how we can *receive* our life vision from God. Each chapter concludes with a set of questions to help you apply the material to your life, or to use as part of a group study.

Paul the apostle believed, achieved, and received God's destiny for him. Near the end of his days on earth, he triumphantly said:

The time has come for me to leave this life.

I have fought the good fight, I have finished
the race, I have kept the faith. Now, a crown
is being held for me—a crown for being right
with God (II Timothy 4:6-8).

Paul made mistakes, committed sins, took wrong
turns, and went through many tests, but before he
died, I believe he had the joy of hearing his Lord and
Savior say:

You did well. You are a good and loyal
servant. Because you were loyal with small
things, I will let you care for much greater
things. Come and share my joy with me (Matthew 25:21).

He had fulfilled his destiny. He had finished his
course. So can you and I. Do you want to know your
place in this world? Are you looking for meaning
and purpose? Do you want to glorify God through
your life?

Then know that you are no accident. You have a
destiny. Your journey of discovery begins by seeing...and believing.

For Thought, Discussion, and Action

1. Do you have a sense of personal destiny? What
   has God called you to do? Share any specifics.

2. Think about or share experiences where God revealed something of your destiny to you. Have
   you obeyed His promptings? What can you do
   today to be obedient to His voice?

3. What people in the Bible besides Paul had a clear
   sense of destiny? How can you be like them?

4. Write down any aspects you have been given of
   God's plan for you. Ask for more as you grow to
   understand what you already have.

2

You Gotta See to Be

Seeing is vital to life. Without clear vision, it's easy to lose direction, stumble, bump into things, and be left unprotected.

I was so nearsighted as a child that the eye doctor recommended contact lenses for me when I was eight years old. Without "aided vision," my nearsightedness was 20/800. (What I saw from 20 feet away, a normal person saw from 800 feet away.)

My wife Shirley still kids me about my poor vision. Even though there's a digital clock with four-inch numbers on a nightstand just a foot-and-a-half from my face, I can't tell what time it is when I take out my lenses at bedtime. One night, I got out of bed and walked right into a wall! Shirley swears that if a burglar ever breaks into our house, she'll have to defend us.

Clear vision is even more important in our spiritual lives. A person can live with poor physical vision by compensating in numerous ways. But what happens when a person has no spiritual vision for his own life?

It's the pits. Life is boring and disjointed. There are many things to stumble over, numerous walls to bump into, and a sickening feeling of powerlessness and frustration. We also learn to compensate, but do it through resignation to circumstances, loneliness, lack of joy and excitement, or silent gnawing pain.

To See or Not to See

Our lives are never greater than our vision. In a sense, what we see is what we are. Shakespeare might have more accurately mused, "To see or not to see; that is the question."

If we "see" God's plan for us, then we can more easily walk the pathway that He brightens before us. Otherwise, we may become lost, and be unprotected prey for the devil.

The thing that stands out most in the lives of godly people in the Bible and history is that they recognized their destiny. They *saw* what God wanted them to do and *trusted Him* to lead them.

- Noah knew his destiny was to build an ark, rescue his family, and begin a new world.

- Abraham saw a vision of a promised land, a nation, and all nations blessed through him.

- Moses knew he would be the deliverer of the Hebrew nation.

- Jeremiah understood his call to be a prophet to the nations.

- John the Baptist knew that God gave him the job of being the forerunner of the Messiah.

- Peter understood his destiny as the pillar of the church and the apostle of the Jews.

These people were just as human as we are. But they became heroes in heaven's eyes, because they were obedient to God's plans. (We will look at this in greater depth in Chapter 13 when we take a stroll through God's Hall of Fame.)

Defining Our Terms

The first American dictionary was compiled in 1828 through the tireless efforts of Noah Webster. It was his desire to give a Christian interpretation to the English language. Webster gave us the following definitions of the words *vision* and *destiny:*

Vision—a revelation from God; something presented supernaturally to the mind; the object of sight.

Destiny—the state or condition appointed or predetermined; invincible necessity; ultimate fate; to set, ordain, or appoint to use.

Webster believed that vision and destiny were crucial to life. Vision came from God, and destiny was ordained by Him.

Throughout this book, we use these two words interchangeably with Webster's original definitions. Modern dictionaries have since changed the meanings. There is no reference to God in them. But to Webster, there was no vision or destiny without God.

Why Vision is So Important

First, when we fulfill the purpose of our creation, the highest honor goes to our Creator.

When filled with flowers, a beautiful vase brings praise to a skilled potter. If the same vase were used to store motor oil in a garage, it would be a waste of the potter's talent.

You and I are vessels made by God for a specific purpose. Jesus revealed a perfect sense of His destiny when He proclaimed in John 17:4, "Having finished the work you gave me to do, I brought you glory on earth."

Second, when each of us does our assigned part, the largest possible harvest of salvation takes place.

You may not have heard of Mordecai Ham. He was called by God to do evangelism in the southern United States during the 1930s. One night in 1934 when he was preaching the Gospel in Charlotte, North Carolina, a teenage boy came forward and gave his life to Christ. That boy was Billy Graham.

Dr. Billy Graham has preached the Gospel to over

69 million people—more than any man in history. But his name would not be a household word if Mordecai Ham hadn't been faithful to God's call. Because he fulfilled his destiny, another link in God's chain of blessing was forged.

Whenever one person is faithful to do God's will, others benefit. We're believers today because someone was faithful to do God's will yesterday.

And third, fulfilling our purpose brings the greatest amount of personal happiness. Nothing is more satisfying than being what you were created to be. Happiness, contentment, and self-worth are by-products of doing God's will for your life.

Yet most kids today are not happy or contented; they are bored stiff. A person is always bored in direct proportion to the degree that he is outside of God's will.

If you're called to be a quarterback, you'll never find happiness as a right tackle. Play your position, and not only will you be fulfilled, but your team will win. That's God's game plan.

Are you bored, confused, anxious, or frustrated about the direction your life is taking? Don't be. God has plans for you. Your process of discovery has already begun. You are just like millions of us who have been educated in a dark world.

Maybe you, too, have *believed in the lie.*

For Thought, Discussion, and Action

1. Why is "spiritual vision" so important? What things tend to block our vision of God's plans?

2. Name three reasons for having a clear sense of vision or destiny. Which is most important? Why do we tend to focus on another one?

3. Think about friends who are bored a lot. Why are they bored? How do you get rid of boredom?

4. Ask God to correct your life vision. Commit yourself to glorify Him, and never be bored again.

3

It's a Lie!

I couldn't believe my eyes. On the front cover of *Time* magazine was a picture of a distinguished-looking, world-renowned scientist standing next to a monkey. The caption over the cover story read, "In the beginning" (a direct quote from Genesis 1:1).

The article said matter-of-factly that scientists now "know" that man was not created by God, but evolved from apes. It stated irreverently that, "In the beginning,"

- There was a Big Bang.
- Then there were planets and galaxies.
- Out of these emerged molecules and compounds.
- Then there was slime.
- It became a fish.
- Then a reptile.
- Next a mammal (all this took time, of course).
- Finally an ape.
- Then it became *you*.

(A friend of mine later summarized this "amazing" process by saying, "From *goo* to *you* by way of the *zoo*.")

Reading it made me sick. What hurt most was the

blatant use of the biblical words "in the beginning" to deny the creation of God.

It reminded me of the time a few years ago when Shirley and I were giving some friends a tour of the Museum of Natural History in Washington, D.C. After looking at displays of the wonders of God's physical universe, we came to a hallway lined with granite pillars. Quotations were etched in stone columns in huge bold-faced lettering. We expected to see uplifting quotations such as Psalm 8:1-3:

Lord our Lord, your name is the most wonderful name in all the earth! ...I look at your heavens, which you made with your fingers. I see the moon and stars, which you created.

Or Jeremiah 32:17:

Oh, Lord God, you made the skies and the earth with your very great power. There is nothing too hard for you to do.

But that's not what was etched on those columns. Instead, we saw quotes from Charles Darwin. His hollow words paid deference to an incredible world without a Creator, a grand design without a Designer.

The Big Lie

The most damaging lie of the past two centuries has been the theory of evolution. Originating with Darwin's *Origin of Species* in 1859, its central creed can be boiled down to this:

Time + Matter + Chance = *You*

To put it another way, three impersonal things (time, matter, and chance) magically produce something wonderfully personal (a human being). We're never told how much time it takes. We aren't told where the matter comes from. We aren't shown how this matter evolves from something so simple to something so complex. Yet millions of people have bought the lie.

The problem is that it's just a theory. It's also not scientific, since by its very nature, science can *never* deal with origins. The greatest problem is that *it's a lie.* A big lie. Plain and simple.

The Bible says it's *not true:*

> In the beginning God created the sky and the earth.
>
> Then God said, "Let us make human beings in our image and likeness."
>
> So God created human beings in his image. In the image of God he created them (Genesis 1:1,26,27).

Belief in the lie has prevented millions of people from discovering their personal destiny and inestimable worth.

For 74 years, the Eastern European nations and the former Soviet Union were held in the totalitarian grip of Communist ideology. For seven decades, children were taught by the state that they were not created by God. In China, over one billion people are still enslaved by communism and its evolutionary underpinnings.

The prevailing humanism of the West promotes the same numbing theory of man's origin. Apathy, disillusionment, and record suicide rates are scathing testimony to the lie.

Though many people reject the most extreme views of evolutionary theory, they are still tainted by it. It has infected us like a philosophical virus, inoculating nearly half the globe with the germs of despair, insignificance, low self-esteem, lack of vision, and meaninglessness.

No idea has damaged the joyous reality of God-given destiny and individual significance more than the lie of evolution. If the universe began with an accidental Big Bang, then your life and mine are meaningless small duds.

Most people think that. And the Bible says, "As

he thinks within himself, so he is" (Proverbs 23:7 NASB).

A Three-fold Deception

The theory of evolution and its destruction of human significance is built on three false premises.

First, evolution says that there is no God nor revelation from Him that tells us of our origins. Charles Darwin was an atheist who had once studied to be a minister. Rejecting God and the Bible, he set out to prove that man was simply the product of natural selection. It plunged him (and all those who follow him) into the abyss of relativity and error.

The Bible states it this way:

> They traded the truth of God for a lie. They worshiped and served what had been created instead of the God who created those things, who should be praised forever (Romans 1:25).

The second lie of evolution is the denial of God's providence. If God doesn't exist (or is so distantly attached to the universe as to be irrelevant), then no one is directing history, and it is determined by the survival of the fittest.

But according to the Bible, God personally guides the affairs of people and nations (Acts 17:26). He is intimately involved in the flow of history.

Third, the lie of evolution discards the special destiny-filled creation of man.

This is where the deception touches us. If there is no God—if He is not involved in His world—then you and I are meaningless blobs of chemical compounds. If godless evolution is true, then life has no purpose, and you and I have no eternal role to play.

Yet the Bible teaches that man is God's special and unique creation who is made in His image (Genesis 1:26,27). We were designed by Him to rule over the earth and to reign with Him one day in heaven (Revelation 22:5). Individually, we are wonderfully made, with a unique destiny and calling (Psalm 139:13-16).

Set Free

Whittaker Chambers was an American atheist and evolutionist who served a number of years ago as the senior editor of *Time* magazine (the same periodical that did the cover story on the scientist and the monkey). After World War I, he married a Communist and threw himself into the Marxist revolution that was then forming in the Soviet Union. In the 1930s, at the height of his career, and while involved as a spy against the U.S. government, he began to have some serious doubts about his godless world view and his lack of personal fulfillment.

One day in 1938, while feeding his small daughter, he was struck by the incredible design and beauty of human life. Here before his eyes was evidence of a personal and loving Creator. She could not be adequately explained through an accumulated series of accidents.

That day, Whittaker Chambers was set free from the lie. Though it would take years to rid himself of his Communist past (and would lead to one of the greatest espionage purges in American history), that one revolutionary day began his pilgrimage toward truth, meaning, and God. Chambers' remarkable story is found in his autobiography called *Witness*.

Something Wonderful

The theory of evolution lacks any shred of truth. The good news is that:

- There is an awesome personal God of the universe who is its creator, sustainer, and redeemer.

- He guides the history of men and nations by His loving actions and commands.

- He made man like Himself—a special order

of creation—with the marks and attributes of His infinite personality.

Each of us needs to reject the lie. The *truth* is:
You are special.
You are wonderfully made.
You have a role to play in God's world.
And as we will see in our next chapter, in God's eyes, you are *beautiful*.

For Thought, Discussion, and Action

1. Why did the devil invent the idea of evolution? Why is it so popular in the West, but not in other parts of the world?

2. How has the theory of evolution affected your own life and thinking? What can you do to transform your mind?

3. Why is evolution wrong? How is it unscientific?

4. Take a stand in your community against the lie of evolution. Speak out in politeness and truth. Tell your friends that an incredible design points to a wonderful Designer.

4

You're Beautiful, Babe

I'm not a fan of television commercials. Occasionally, though, one comes along that really touches the heart.

A few years ago, David, our lovable five-year-old, brought one to my attention. Bounding into my lap, he rattled off a commercial for the television show "Who's the Boss." When he came to the sentimental punch line, he grabbed my arms, smiled up into my eyes, and uttered the catchwords, "You're beautiful, babe." Pulling him closer, I said, "You're beautiful, too, Davy."

For the next few months, when one of us needed encouragement, we repeated those words, "You're beautiful, babe." They convey a powerful idea, the way God feels about everything He has created.

God thinks that we are beautiful, special, and wonderful. He ought to know. He's the one who made us.

Beauty Is in the Eye of the Beholder

A good place to take a warm, daily scriptural bath is in the soothing revelational waters of Psalm 139. In it, David describes God's view of His creation of every living person:

> You made my whole being; you formed me
> in my mother's body. I praise you because you
> made me in an amazing and wonderful way.
> What you have done is *wonderful. I know this*

very well. You saw my bones being formed as I took shape in my mother's body. When I was put together there, you saw my body as it was formed. All the days planned for me were written in your book before I was one day old.

God, your thoughts are precious to me. They are so many! If I could count them, they would be more than all the grains of sand. When I wake up, I am still with you (Psalm 139:13-18, italics mine).

This passage describes God's view of the earthly beginnings of each one of us. Peering into his mother's womb through the eyes of God, David was struck by wonder that:

- God was the one who carefully formed each of us (v.13).
- He did it in an utterly amazing way (v.14).
- He watched over every detail of the process (vv.15,16).
- Every day of our lives was planned (v.16).
- God's loving thoughts toward us are greater than all the grains of sand in the world (v.18).

What an incredible revelation about our beginnings! What sometimes seemed like just a wearying nine-month marathon for Mom was actually the making of a masterpiece by God. David said that he understood this truth *very well*. No wonder he was a man with a sense of destiny.

A Mixed-up View of Beauty

The world has a strange concept of beauty. From Barbie to Miss America, the message seems to be that beauty lies in conformity.

That's why in the 1960s, all the girls wanted straight hair and thin bodies (remember Twiggy?). In the next decade, curly came "in" (inspired by

Farrah Fawcett), and everyone bought a curling iron. Men wore long hair in the 1960s and 1970s. Then they returned to short hair (moussed, of course) for the 1980s and 1990s.

But it all boiled down to one thing: to be beautiful, you had to look a certain way. It helped if you were born a bit good-looking, but one could always fall back on estrogen, collagen, or plastic surgery.

Unfortunately, that left the average person with a number of problems:

- The majority of us were not born with all the natural attributes our culture deems beautiful.

- Even if we looked "better than most," the standard of beauty kept changing.

- Most of us couldn't afford the clothes, let alone the treatments, to stay in the race.

So most of us just concluded that we weren't beautiful. And the older we got, the more we decided it wasn't even worth the effort. We'd settle for a normal, ugly life.

Beautifully You

But God's concept of beauty is different. Your uniqueness makes you beautiful to Him. He deliberately made only one of you. He gave you the skin color He wanted you to have; He gave you the build of His choice; He gave you a temperament, personality, and physical makeup unlike anyone else.

He gave you a special smile, a unique frown, and a laugh tailored to your personality. He chose the color of your eyes and hair. He even numbered the hairs on your head.

He did this with everything He created. No two snowflakes are alike, no two rocks, no stars in the sky, no blades of grass.

In all the universe, God's concept of beauty is

based upon individuality. Our differences in race, temperament, and gifts are our glory, not a point of competition. He doesn't want a world of Barbie dolls. He wants you, and He wants me. He made each one of us beautiful in our uniqueness.

Along with that comes an individually crafted destiny. No wonder David could exclaim:

The Lord is all I need. He takes care of me.
My share in life has been pleasant; *my part has been beautiful.*

I praise the Lord because he advises me.
So I rejoice and am glad (Psalm 16:5,6,7,9, italics mine).

As I write, Shirley and I and our four children anxiously await the arrival of Baby Boehme Number Five. It's been six years since we've had a little tyke around the house. Megan, our blonde, vivacious six-year-old, has informed everyone that it will be a girl. She reasoned that since the baby is in Mommy's tummy, it must be a girl. She said that if the baby were in Daddy's tummy, it would be a boy!

During Shirley's pregnancy, we have thought and prayed about the wonder of what is taking place so quietly and amazingly inside her womb. We've felt the kicks and noticed the incredible growth. We've seen God at work.

We've also felt deep sadness to think of the millions of beautifully destined human beings who are killed in their mother's womb through the evil of abortion. What a tragic loss of beauty to the world.

You Must Have Been a Beautiful Baby

What's true of our expected baby was also true of you. Years ago, God chose a time and place to bring you into his plans for planet earth. He wanted to add someone unique and wonderful to the race of man. His idea was *you.*

For a moment, take yourself back to those precious beginning days in your mother's womb. Using material from Gary Bergel's booklet, *When You Were Formed in Secret*, let's imagine what God was up to when He decided it was time to create *you*....

You began when the sperm cell from your father united with the egg cell of your mother. These two particular cells were chosen by God out of millions that participated in the process. God breathed into these chosen cells the gift of life. At this moment of conception, you were smaller than a grain of sand. From two tiny cells, you would explode over some 266 days into a newborn baby weighing approximately seven-and-a-half pounds and containing millions and millions of cells.

God linked together 23 chromosomes from the mother with 23 chromosomes from the father, each set carrying 15,000 genes from each parent cell. The color of your eyes, hair, and skin; facial features; body type; and qualities of personality and intelligence were determined by His skillful choices.

While causing the cells of your new being to multiply, He gently led you down your mother's Fallopian tube to His workshop in the womb. There He gently implanted you in the soft wall of a uterus which had been specially prepared by a hormone called progesterone. Over the next weeks, God would "signal" your mother that you were there by causing her to miss a menstrual period.

He then continued His skillful work by creating a bubbly sac in which to protect and insulate you, and creating an engineering marvel in the umbilical cord to feed you food and oxygen.

Each day, He rapturously created more of you at a dizzying rate of speed. He laughed at three weeks as your tiny heart took its first beat. On your 24th day, you had no arms or legs. Before a month had gone by, He carefully crafted your limbs, backbone, spinal column, and nervous system. By the end of four weeks, He had molded you into a marvelous being that was 10,000 times your original size.

During your second and third months of life, the Master Craftsman worked on your incredible features. He delicately formed your nose, lips, and tongue. He moved muscle cells into position, and soon, 40 sets of muscles began their first exercises. He lengthened your arms to be as long as printed exclamation marks, and carefully formed your fingers and toes, complete with fingerprints to give you a unique identity for the rest of your life.

As your eyelids closed, as thin as butterfly wings, and as God covered you with a translucent skin, you assumed an ethereal, transcendent beauty. You slept. You awoke. From six weeks on, God gave you the ability to experience the sensation of pain. He shed His first tears over you as He thought about the pains of life you would encounter on the way to your heavenly home.

For the next few months, the Lord God developed and refined your unique characteristics at an astonishing rate of speed. Your umbilical cord was then transporting 300 quarts of fluid a day, at speeds up to four miles an hour. It was as if the Master could not wait for you to burst upon His world.

You heard your mother's voice for the first time. You sucked your thumb. Meanwhile, the Lord set your oil and sweat glands into motion, and began to cover you with a white, greasy-looking ointment called vernix, to protect your skin from the amniotic fluid. Your eyes opened. God smiled as the first rays of dim light entered your being.

During the final three months, your loving Creator carefully prepared you for entrance into this world. Finishing touches were added to your rapidly growing features. He thickened and polished your skin, preparing it for the 30- to 40-degree drop in temperature that you would encounter at birth. He carefully stored a layer of fat beneath your skin, for insulation and as a food supply. Approximately one week before Day 260, He lovingly turned your head downward into the pelvic cavity.

His masterpiece was now ready. Beginning your mother's labor pains (a reminder of the consequence of Eve's original sin), He put away His tools, looked lovingly and hopefully at your waiting face, and gave the signal. Angels gathered at your side. Humans scurried about, readying a room for the experience called delivery.

You were now ready for the miracle of birth. God smiled with the breadth of eternal understanding. What He had made was good.

Believe It

God wants each of us to recognize the wonder of our creation and to *believe* that we've been created by amazing design and loving foresight. When He gave you the spark of life, and exploded you into existence from two cells to millions and millions of cells, He smiled...worked...mused...and rejoiced that you were different from any other being He'd ever created. And surely He must have whispered,

"You're beautiful, babe."

For Thought, Discussion, and Action

1. How does the world view beauty? Give examples. How does God's concept of beauty differ?

2. What features or characteristics (physical and spiritual) are unique to you? Do you hate them or appreciate them? Why?

3. Think about the wonder of the nine months in which God fashioned you inside your mother. Meditate on Psalm 139.

4. Go to a mirror. Smile at God's wonderfully unique creation, and say, "You're beautiful, babe!"

5

Aim High, Shoot Long

Now that we recognize God has a plan for each of us, our next step is to discover His specific call on our lives. It's one thing to be excited about the adventure that lies ahead; it's another to be committed to going the distance.

Numbering Our Days

For the past few years, I've been accused of being a fanatic with a calculator. It all started one day when I was meditating on Psalm 90, the song of Moses, and came across these words:

> The length of our days is seventy years— or eighty, if we have the strength; yet their span is but trouble and sorrow; for they quickly pass, and we fly away. Who knows the power of your anger? For your wrath is as great as the fear that is due you. Teach us to number our days aright, that we may gain a heart of wisdom. May the favor of the Lord our God rest upon us; establish the work of our hands for us—yes, establish the work of our hands (Psalm 90:10-12,17 NIV).

"Teach us to number our days...." Those words seemed to jump off the page at me. Our days are truly numbered. Moses lived to be 120 years old. In this great psalm, uttered most certainly toward the end of his life, he reflected on the brevity of life, and how important it is to use our limited days wisely.

I thought of an interview I'd seen on television. A group of people in their 80s were asked what the most important lesson they'd learned about life was. To a person, they all yelled out, "How short it is!"

Moses felt the same way. Though he had already lived longer than most people of his time, and had fulfilled God's calling on his life, the cry of his heart remained, "Teach me to number my days that I might gain a heart of wisdom."

I pulled out my calculator. If I lived out my lifetime, how many days might there actually be? Taking into account the life spans of my parents and grandparents, and using other related factors, I surmised that I could realistically live for 85 years.

My life span could be from 1953 to 2038. I figured out the number of days. Roughly 31,046 (counting leap years).

Next, I figured out how many days I had already lived. I had 17,804 left. Over half of my life was ahead of me. Getting caught up in this, I calculated a few other possibilities:

- My days as a Christian on earth—25,936 (or 71 years).

- Days of marriage—22,651 (or 62 years).
  Shirley smiled when I showed this to her.

- Number of descendants we would produce —15,625 (what potential to bless the world!).

Then I decided to do something radical. In order to literally "number my days," I began to record in my daily journal the number of days that I had lived, and the number of days I might have left.

As I write, my figures stand at: 14,157 days lived, 16,868 possible days left. Numbered and counting.

The Importance of Perspective

This simple revelation from Psalm 90 greatly changed my life and ministry. Though I realized I could easily be wrong on the actual length of my life, the concept of numbering my days helped me make wise decisions. When your days are numbered, you want to make each one count.

It also brings to mind that famous saying: "One small life will soon be past. Only what's done for Christ will last."

Apocalyptic Vision

One of the great problems of our day is the narrow, short-term, escape-oriented perspective that many Christians have on their lives. This is primarily due to the saturation of "end-times" teaching that has blanketed the Church for years. We've been told that the end of the world is before us, or that Jesus is coming soon, or that the Tribulation will be here any day.

It is beyond the scope of this book to speculate as to when the Rapture will happen or when the Tribulation will begin. In my book *Leadership for the 21st Century*, a chapter is devoted to this subject. Its simple thesis is that we need to stay ready for Christ's return, while not neglecting our Kingdom responsibilities over the course of our lifetime.

Because of this "last-days" emphasis, many believers are schizophrenic regarding long-range vision for their lives. In their practical, everyday world, they've been taught to plan for retirement, set aside money to pay for their children's education, and bank enough extra cash to cover emergencies. Many look forward to receiving Social Security checks.

In their spiritual lives, it's just the opposite. They live for today, and wait for Jesus to return.

We need to balance end-time readiness with long-range planning. Every spring, I think of this when we plant a garden behind our house. When you plant a garden, all you have to start with is dirt.

But you can envision the end results: lush cucumbers, rows of bushy carrot tops, and corn stalks swaying in the wind.

Before that becomes a reality, the soil needs to be tilled and enriched. Seeds need to be sowed. The garden needs weeding, watering, and sunlight.

Our lives are like a garden. If we don't expect the garden to grow, we will neglect to nourish it. If we don't have long-term vision, we won't sow the seeds today that will bring the rich harvest tomorrow.

Aim High

If we are to be the people God designed us to be, then we've got to set our goals high. Someone once said, "Most people aim at nothing and hit it."

When my dad was teaching me to play golf, he used to say, "Never up, never in," meaning that if you don't hit the ball far enough, it'll never go in the hole. Being an amateur at the game, I ignored his advice. I usually putted the ball short of the hole.

The same is true of the game of life. If we don't set our sights high, then we will certainly settle for something less than our best.

Shoot Long

In order for your spiritual dreams to come true, you must have the desire to go the distance. This is where the numbering of your days takes on exciting dimensions.

How many years might you expect to live if Jesus doesn't return soon? What things does He want you to accomplish during those years? What do you need to do right now in order to accomplish them?

When the revelation of Psalm 90 sank deeply into my soul, I sat down and listed some lifetime goals in the areas of devotion, ministry, evangelism, writing (including this book), and other projects. I committed myself afresh to my wife, our children, and the 15,000 descendants who would come from us. Those commitments are now prayerfully stored in a heart that desires to fulfill God's will.

Ready, Aim....

Now it's your turn.
Get out your calculator.
Number your days.
Aim high and shoot long.
Then begin planting those seeds.

For Thought, Discussion, and Action

1. Why do people plan for college and retirement, but give very little thought to God's long-range spiritual plans for their lives? Have you done this? How can you change it?

2. Where are you at in the planting of your "life's garden"? Tilling soil? Planting seeds? Reaping fruit? Being hoed?

3. What plans can you make for one year—five years—twenty years—that will help you to fulfill your life's destiny? List them on paper. Share them with others.

4. Get out your calculator. How many days have you lived (remember to count leap years)? How many days might you have left? Allow this long-range focus to bring healthy change to your life and priorities.

Section II

You Have a Destiny—Achieve It

For this very reason, make every effort to add to your faith goodness; and to goodness, knowledge; and to knowledge, self-control; and to self-control, perseverance; and to perseverance, godliness; and to godliness, brotherly kindness; and to brotherly kindness, love. For if you possess these qualities in increasing measure, they will keep you from being ineffective and unproductive in your knowledge of our Lord Jesus Christ. Therefore, my brothers, be all the more eager to make your calling and election sure. For if you do these things, you will never fall, and you will receive a rich welcome into the eternal kingdom of our Lord and Savior Jesus Christ (II Peter 1:5-8,10,11 NIV, italics mine).

The Greeks said that character is destiny. The Bible agrees with this in II Peter 1 when it lists seven character qualities which are essential to a fruitful and productive life.

These dynamic character qualities will make our lives effective and productive (v.8), and our calling sure (v.10). They will keep us from falling (v.10), and will secure our future in God's eternal Kingdom (v.11).

In the following section, we will examine in depth how each of these characteristics can be achieved in your life. Without them, your destiny cannot be realized. With them, God promises that you *cannot fail* to be who you were created to be.

6

Be Good

While training to play on a national basketball team which would tour the South Pacific during the summer of 1970, I heard a message that caused me to look at life in a different way.

Steve Patterson, starting center for the UCLA Bruins, and the man who was later that year to lead his team to their fifth straight national championship, spoke to us one evening around a campfire.

UCLA was in its golden era of basketball dominance, eventually winning national titles ten out of twelve years. The team's coach was a well-known Christian, the legendary "wizard of Westwood," John Wooden. Steve shared with us Coach Wooden's philosophy.

"Did you know," Steve began, "that at UCLA we never scout the teams we're going to play next?" You could almost hear a gasp.

"Coach Wooden says that it's not important what the other teams do or what superstars they have. He believes that if we master the essentials of the sport, then we can beat any team in America."

He went on to describe how his team perfected dribbling, passing, and shooting. And then he finished by reiterating his main point: "Coach Wooden has taught us that the key to success is majoring in the fundamentals."

When the campfire broke up and I returned to my

cabin, I was still thinking about what I had heard that night: *master the essentials; major in fundamentals*

That summer, our team took those words to heart as we traveled throughout the Pacific Rim, going 29-1. When I returned home, I made a commitment to apply this principle to other areas of my life.

Majoring in Majors

God's word abounds with the need to master the basics. No clearer passage can be found than in II Peter 1, where the famous apostle names seven fundamental qualities of character that are essential to a fulfilled life. Peter tells us to add to our faith (our entrance into God's Kingdom), the following:

- goodness
- knowledge
- self-control
- perseverance
- godliness
- kindness
- love

These are basic; they are simple and attainable.

Many people today major in minors. They waste time scouting out the enemy. They look for superstars to emulate. They chase elaborate doctrinal schemes. And they fall flat on their faces.

God promises us (read the entire context of II Peter 1:2-11) that if we just master the fundamentals, we will:

- never be useless (v.8)
- know the Lord and have better lives (v.8)
- never fall (v.10)
- receive a rich welcome into His eternal Kingdom (v.11)

In the following chapters, we will consider each of these more closely. Let's begin with goodness.

Inner Purity

It is no coincidence that Peter says, first of all, to add goodness to our faith.

The most important character trait of our lives is heart purity, inner virtue, integrity, or in a simple word—*goodness*. When we first come to Christ, our greatest problem is sin. We have been thoroughly polluted by selfishness. Our motives are wrong. Our inner being has been defiled. Our heart has been darkened. When we give our lives to Christ, He immediately begins a massive "moral toxic waste" clean-up operation.

Without a pure heart, we can proceed no further. There is too much rubble and junk in the way. So we begin the process of moral renovation by adding goodness to our faith.

Past, Present, and Future

In I Timothy 1:5, Paul says that the goal of all spiritual instruction—all teaching, sermons, books, video tapes, audio cassettes, or other methods of communicating truth—is to produce loving people.

He then tells us that what is necessary to be a loving person is to have a pure heart, a good conscience, and a true faith. These three elements give an excellent definition of the character quality of goodness. Let's examine them individually.

A Pure Heart

Heart purity describes a *present* state of being. It involves analyzing our thoughts and motives, allowing the Lord to search our hearts and minds, and keeping ourselves free of sin at all times.

Many years ago, I began the practice of taking daily accounts. I started by kneeling by my bed at night and opening up my life to the Lord in the attitude of Psalm 139:23,24:

God, examine me and know my heart; test me and know my nervous thoughts. See if there is any bad thing in me. Lead me on the road to everlasting life.

Usually, I asked the Lord some questions about my heart and let Him reveal His thoughts to me. Did I demonstrate any pride in my life today? Did I doubt Him in any area? Was I disobedient? Was I unloving to any person?

Then I let Him speak. Where there was conviction, I asked forgiveness. Where there was no perceived guilt, I offered thanks.

Today I try to keep my heart pure on a moment-to-moment basis. Christian maturity is, after all, shortening the time period between sin and confession, revelation and obedience. Since sin is our main problem (Romans 3:23), we want to get rid of it as soon as possible. When our hearts are right with God to the best of our ability, we will know deep and abiding peace.

A Good Conscience

A few years after my Christian sports trip, I attended a large seminar in Seattle put on by Bill Gothard of the Institute of Basic Life Principles.

Before 18,000 people, Mr. Gothard explained the importance of having a good conscience before God. He shared his experience of asking God to show him what people in his past he had sinned against and to whom he now needed to make confession and/or restitution for his sins. His list came to 20.

He went on to share very candidly what freedom had come to his life when he made all of these past relationships right (to the best of his ability). He then turned to the audience and said:

If each of you will clear your conscience of past sins, and if the average list of people you need to make things right with is around 20, then very soon 360,000 people in Seattle will hear a humble testimony of how Jesus can change lives. Also, you will be set free from the guilt of the past.

His words cut deeply into my soul, and my mind began to race. If we all confessed our past sins, 360,000 people will hear about Christ! My mind began to compute. That was two-thirds of the entire city of Seattle. And freedom will come to my own life if I take care of my sins of the past.

I determined to give it a try. One day, while holed up in the seclusion of my grandparents' waterfront home, I patiently (and agonizingly) listed on paper all of the past sins I could ever remember committing. I used the helpful guide in chapter three of Charles Finney's *Revival Lectures*. (A reprint of that guide, entitled *Break Up Your Fallow Ground*, may be ordered from Last Days Ministries, P.O. Box 40, Lindale, TX 75771.)

After five hours, and three "goings-over," the list numbered roughly 300 specific acts of sin (that I could remember), and 15 to 20 people whom I needed to make things right with.

I thanked God for His grace and love, then burned the piece of paper in the fireplace, with tears streaming down my cheeks. In the coming days, I followed through and cleared my conscience of the sins of the past. It was like taking a spiritual shower that made me feel clean all over.

A clear conscience is crucial for inner freedom and holiness. It removes all the skeletons of the past that the enemy loves to drag out to haunt us.

True Faith

We've seen that inner purity—or goodness—involves maintaining a pure heart in the *present* and clearing away the sins of the *past*. It also involves having a hope-filled faith in the *future*.

True faith is really a by-product of meticulously taking care of the first two rules. It is this sincere faith which is ultimately most "pleasing to God" (Hebrews 11:6).

A Final Warning

Purity of heart is especially important when it comes to sexual sin and its motivation of lust. Goodness nourishes. Lust rots. In II Peter 1:4, we are told that we can either be "partakers of God's nature"—literally, feed on God—or we can be eaten up by lust.

Ask basketball star Magic Johnson. He possessed many admirable character traits, but he was bound by lust and impurity, and is slowly dying from AIDS

Ask boxer Mike Tyson. His lustful heart landed him in prison.

Be Good

The number-one character goal of our lives must be holiness of heart. Jesus said in Matthew 5:8, "Those who are pure in their thinking are happy, because they will be with God."

The apostle Paul stated, "We should make ourselves pure—free from anything that makes body or soul unclean" (II Corinthians 7:1).

King David added years before, "Who may go up on the mountain of the Lord? Who may stand in his holy temple? Only those with clean hands and pure hearts" (Psalm 24:3,4).

And the writer to the Hebrews warned, "Try to live in peace with all people, and try to live free from sin. Anyone whose life is not holy will never see the Lord" (Hebrews 12:14).

In our next chapter, we will take a look at the second pillar of sound character, knowledge.

For Thought, Discussion, and Action

1. Why is goodness or virtue the beginning point in our building of strong character? What happens when we fail to have good hearts? Give some personal or historical examples.

2. Have you purified your heart by clearing your conscience of all known past sin? When did you do it? If not, when will you do it?

3. Which do you have a greater problem with: A pure heart? A good conscience? Or a sincere faith? Discuss what can be done to strengthen you in your area of weakness.

4. Purify your heart daily. Clean up the past. Smile at the future. Be honest about sexual temptation, and have others pray for you in this area. Be good.

7

Learn

When goodness is established in our heart, we can turn our attention to our mind. Peter says in the second half of II Peter 1:5, "and to goodness, [add] knowledge."

Goodness first; *knowledge* second. Notice the order. That's the way God designed it. Every school, college, and university should be established on this principle. Separating goodness of character from the pursuit of knowledge can end up tragically.

Knowledge can become a curse instead of a blessing if it's not used with a pure heart. Two examples from history will serve to illustrate this point.

A Philosopher and a King

Friedrich Nietzsche (1844-1900) had one of the greatest minds in history. Receiving his doctorate in philosophy from the University of Leipzig in 1869, he spent a major portion of his life teaching in Basel, Switzerland, and writing from his chalet in the beautiful village of Sils Maria.

Though he had a brilliant mind and great breadth of knowledge, Nietzsche was an immoral man, engaging in numerous adulterous relationships. His lustful heart molded a deceived intellect that was the first in the modern era to say that God is dead. His concepts of "supermen" and the "will to power" greatly influenced both the rise of Nazism in his home country and Marxism in Russia.

In 1869, Nietzsche had a breakdown, and ultimately went insane. He died of syphilis on August
25, 1900. Though his mind was brilliant, his impure
heart drove him to error, insanity, and finally death.

Solomon is called the wisest man who ever lived
(I Kings 3:12). In the earlier years of his life, he
followed the example of his father David, walking
with God and maintaining a good heart before Him.
As long as he obeyed God, he was blessed with
wisdom, knowledge, riches, and stature.

Sometime during his reign, Solomon's heart
began to turn away from God through the lustful
pursuit of foreign women whom he took as wives (I
Kings 11:1-6). As his heart descended into the darkness of lust and idol worship, his mind became confused and depressed. Toward the end of his life, in
total mental despair, Solomon cried out in the writing of Ecclesiastes:

> Useless! Useless! Completely useless! Ev-
> erything is useless....So I decided to find out
> about wisdom and knowledge and also about
> foolish thinking, but this turned out to be like
> chasing the wind.

> But then I looked at what I had done, and
> I thought about all the hard work. Suddenly I
> realized it was useless, like chasing the wind
> (excerpts from Ecclesiastes 1,2).

Both Nietzsche and King Solomon—separated by
nearly 2,000 years of history—made tragic mistakes.
They thought they could be wise without the protection of a godly heart. They were wrong. Knowledge,
without goodness, only makes men miserable. If
your heart is wrong, you cannot use knowledge in
satisfying and beneficial ways to the glory of God.

How's Your Receiver?

Knowledge is the second pillar in our house of
Christian discipleship. In this chapter, we will not

primarily focus on *what* God wants us to know, but on *how* He wants us to bring wisdom into our lives. The Bible calls it "being strong in spirit" (Luke 1:80).

The human mind is the instrument God uses to disclose to us the wonders of His being and His creation. It's like a radio receiver tuned in to receive transmissions directly from God.

If our mind isn't working to full capacity—like a radio receiver with severed or frayed wires—then our "reception" of what He sends will be poor, regardless of how hard He tries to reach us.

The human mind works like a muscle. It maintains its health through exercise. The more we use it, the stronger it will become. Like a muscle, if we neglect to use it properly, it will become weak.

There are three practical ways we can strengthen our minds.

Be a Thinker

We need to use our minds. Many people don't like that idea. We've grown so used to living by our feelings that critical, reasoned thought sounds like work. "Tell me what to do, but don't ask me to think," has become a common cry.

Through rejecting God, modern man has become like Solomon. Thinking makes us sad (Ecclesiastes 1:17), because we're lost and confused. So we've sidetracked that incredible mind that God has given us, and have allowed the engine of our emotions to pull the train.

As an example, the United States Supreme Court changed thousands of years of revelation and clear thinking with the stroke of a pen by condoning abortion on demand (the infamous Roe v. Wade decision) on January 22, 1973. Abortion had been considered the most hideous of crimes for more than 4,000 years. To any reasonable mind, it was wrong legally, morally, medically, scientifically, ethically, and socially. Yet, except for a small segment of the Catholic

Church and a few conservative activists, most American Christians didn't even blink.

Paul mentions the importance of a strong and thoughtful mind to our overall Christian lives when he says:

> Do not change yourselves to be like the people of this world, but be changed within *by a new way of thinking*. Then you will be able to decide what God wants for you; you will know what is good and pleasing to him and what is perfect (Romans 12:2, italics mine).

We can develop clear and forceful minds by:

- Asking questions as we read God's word.

- Contemplating and pondering the issues of our day.

- Talking and reasoning with God and His people.

- Being diligent to study and look for answers.

- Maintaining curiosity and inquisitiveness.

- Always asking, seeking, and knocking.

Be a Reader

I remember a book a few years ago called *Why Johnny Can't Read*. It described the 150-year decline of reading skills in the United States, and the dramatic results of illiteracy. The problem was that very few people read the book.

Reading is vital to learning. It probably has no equal as a communicator. It focuses attention, reveals clearly (in black and white), allows time for meditation (you control the speed), encourages logical thinking, and even teaches spelling and grammar. God's primary method of transmitting information to man has been through the written word—the Bible, showing the high value He places on reading.

The devil knows this. He uses illiteracy for his own purposes. If people are unable to read, they can't read the Bible. Also, he knows that if he can discourage those who are able to read by keeping them from enjoying it, he can keep them away from the knowledge of God.

What made Ezra a great leader in Israel?

> Ezra...was a teacher, knew well the Teachings of Moses that had been given by the Lord....had worked hard to know and obey the Teachings of the Lord and to teach his rules and commands (Ezra 7:6,10).

What was one of the secrets of Timothy's walk with God?

> You should continue following the teachings you learned....Since you were a child you have known the Holy Scriptures which are able to make you wise. And that wisdom leads to salvation through faith in Christ Jesus (II Timothy 3:14,15).

All great leaders have been readers. It's been true in history, and is especially true today in the age of rapidly changing information, that you must read to lead. This starts with our commitment to the best book of all—the Bible.

A few years ago, I realized that I was not growing in certain areas of my life, because I was not taking time to read. Work, pleasure, television, and other distractions had crowded in. I decided to start reading again, and came up with three new concepts.

First, I needed to meditate on and digest the material I read. Second, I needed to master a few books rather than to scan many. And finally, I needed to read the best books available related to my gifts and calling.

Some years ago, I helped launch a program called "Read-to-Lead." This program provides the very best in Christian literature to those willing to read.

For more information, write to Renewal Communications, Read-to-Lead Program, 6830 Arlington Pl. S.E., Port Orchard, WA 98366.

Be a Writer

We now turn to the third area that is vital to growing in knowledge. Francis Bacon once said, "Reading maketh a full man; conference a ready man; and writing an exact man."

Writing has been man's main form of passing information from one generation to another. How grateful we should be that the writers of the books of the Bible valued the written form.

Writing is an important discipline, and is an invaluable tool to gain thorough understanding. If you don't enjoy writing, you can develop the skill by taking notes wherever you go, especially when you're in a setting where God's truth is being shared.

Then rewrite your notes. I learned this from a biology teacher when I was a freshman in college. He told his students that he could guarantee them a good grade if they would simply rewrite their notes from his class. It forces you to organize and remember what you have heard better.

A final aspect of writing that has a multitude of benefits is the practice of keeping a spiritual diary or journal on a regular basis. I've been keeping a spiritual journal for 20 years now. It helps me to see how God is working in my life right at the moment. It reminds me of guidance or direction He has given me in the past. It allows me to recall His miracles and faithfulness. And it will provide a lasting testimony to my friends and family.

The Treasure of Knowledge

The Bible likens wisdom and knowledge to a precious treasure, to be sought after and guarded at all cost (Proverbs 3:13-26). We have seen the importance of developing the disciplines of thinking, reading, and writing. With virtuous hearts and minds filled with knowledge, we are on our way to achieving our highest potential and protecting our cherished freedoms.

Samuel Adams, one of America's founders, must have been reading II Peter 1:5 when he said:

> While the People are virtuous they cannot be subdued; but when once they lose their Virtue they will be ready to surrender their Liberties to the first external or internal invader...*If Virtue and Knowledge are diffused among the People, they will never be enslaved. This will be their great Security* (italics mine).

For Thought, Discussion, and Action

1. Why must goodness precede knowledge in God's university of life? What happens to smart people who have bad hearts? Give some examples.

2. What are the three things you can do to strengthen and exercise your mind for the task of learning? In which of the three are you weak? In which are you strong?

3. How many books do you read a month? A year? What new goals are you going to set for yourself to grow in grace and knowledge?

4. Join the Read-to-Lead program. Commit yourself to be a good thinker, reader, and writer for God.

8

Control Yourself

Our world seems ripe to learn some self-control following years of:

- sex scandals involving politicians
- fallen television evangelists
- professional athletes with AIDS
- serial killers
- rioting in the streets
- abused children, date rapes, battered wives
- mountains of evidence of an entire culture falling apart.

It is reported that James Madison, the fourth president of the United States, said nearly two hundred years ago:

We have staked the whole future of American civilization, not upon the power of government, far from it. We have staked the future of all of our political institutions upon the capacity of mankind for self-government; upon the capacity of each and all of us to govern ourselves, *to control ourselves*, to sustain ourselves according to the Ten Commandments of God (italics mine).

Failure to obey God's commands in our daily lives has brought anarchy and havoc. Self-control is a pillar of a free society.

As we've seen in previous chapters, Christlike character begins in the heart with goodness, and then goes to the mind through knowledge. Next, it is rooted in the will through self-control.

We are told in II Peter 1:6, "to knowledge, [add] self-control."

Self-control is sometimes regarded as a negative thing. I'm sure many of you can relate to some of the misconceptions of my early childhood.

"Don't Touch Those Cookies!"

I remember coming home from school and often being faced with a true test of self-control. As soon as I'd get in the house, I'd be hit with the smell of freshly baked chocolate chip cookies.

Racing into the kitchen, I would see a plate of them sitting on the counter. Mom was usually nearby, cleaning up messy pans.

"Don't touch those cookies," she would say.

It was like a shot to the stomach.

It took all the self-control I could muster to keep my grubby little hands off those cookies.

Sometimes, when she left the room, I'd "borrow a cookie." If I got caught, my parents showed me another form of control called "shelf control," in which they applied a hairbrush to my bottom shelf!

Possessing Right

My concept of self-control was backward. I thought self-control was "resisting temptation or evil." Later in life, I discovered that this is not the proper emphasis. Self-control is not primarily resisting wrong. It is *possessing right with such conviction that resisting wrong is the natural result.*

We're born with a bent toward evil, which theologians call moral depravity. Simply stated, it's easy to do wrong. Wrong pulls us along like gravity. For instance, it's easy to run downhill than it is to run uphill. (I'm reminded of this every day during my morning jog.) The key to going against the pull is a conviction that the hill is worth climbing.

When we're committed to holy living, the resistance to temptation becomes an automatic response to a choice already made. That's why goodness in the heart must precede self-control.

Learn to Control Your Tongue

Our ability to communicate through speech is a wonderful gift. Our words are also one of the places we are most often tested. Who among us is perfect in our words?

James said that nobody except Jesus is perfect.

We all make many mistakes. If people never said anything wrong, they would be perfect and able to control their entire selves, too. When we put bits into the mouths of horses to make them obey us, we can control their whole bodies. Also a ship is very big, and it is pushed by strong winds. But a very small rudder controls that big ship, making it go wherever the pilot wants. It is the same with the tongue. It is a small part of the body, but it brags about great things.

A big forest fire can be started with only a little flame. And the tongue is like a fire....The tongue is set on fire by hell, and it starts a fire that influences all of life (James 3:2-6).

How true. All of us say things we wish we could take back. A friend of mine once said that every time he spoke, he put his foot in his mouth. He said he opened his mouth again only to change feet.

Whether it's taking God's name in vain, lying (including fibs or "little white lies"), speaking before we think, telling jokes at someone else's expense, using sarcasm that hurts, or lashing out in anger, we've all been guilty of not controlling our tongues.

Jesus said that "God will hold us responsible one

day for *every careless word we have said*" (Matthew 12:36, italics mine). That's a strong enough incentive to make sure that what we say will "always be with grace, seasoned, as it were, with salt, so that you may know how you should respond to each person" (Colossians 4:6 NASB).

Begin your development of self-control with the greatest challenge—your speech. Commit yourself to absolute honesty. Be quick to listen and slow to respond. Always seek to build up, never to tear down. You will never be perfect. But you can increase your awareness of the power of words.

Control Your Conduct

While changing planes in Chicago, I couldn't help noticing a group of young people in the same waiting room. They slouched on chairs, wrestled on the carpet, threw spit wads and paper airplanes, and made general nuisances of themselves.

I was embarrassed by their poor example. I'd traveled enough to know that the "ugly American" image was often earned.

Our entire culture needs a good lesson in behavioral self-control. Paul said to his young friend Timothy many years ago, "Be an example to the believers with your words, your actions, your love, your faith, and your pure life" (I Timothy 4:12).

Another way to say this is, "Don't talk the talk until you're willing to walk the walk."

The choice to control our actions, according to the commandments of God, is a decision we have to make constantly. The right choices can only be made if, out of our love and commitment to Jesus, we "want to do right more than anything else" (Matthew 5:6). We have a choice of:

- the awe and respect we show for God.

- the honor and obedience we give our parents.

- the ways we relate to siblings and friends.
- the body language we use.
- the way we groom and dress ourselves.
- the manners we show toward others.
- the rights of others that we honor and promote.

For the past 40 years, Western culture has been sliding down the mountain of self-control each year. It shows up most in youth culture. From Elvis in the 1950s to Madonna in the 1990s, we have barreled down the hill until a total lack of restraint has become the accepted norm.

As Christians, we need to aim for the highest standards. We need to choose daily to govern ourselves by the principles of God's Word. In the words of the apostle James:

Are there those among you who are truly wise and understanding? Then they should show it by *living right* and doing good things with a gentleness that comes from wisdom....But the wisdom that comes from God is first of all pure, then peaceful, gentle, and easy to please. This wisdom is always ready to help those who are troubled and to do good for others. It is always fair and honest. People who work for peace in a peaceful way plant a good crop of right-living (James 3:13,17,18, italics mine).

Learn to Control Your Time

A final area of much-needed self-control is in the effective use of time. In fact, no area more clearly shows our sense of godly perspective than the way we use the precious minutes that God has given us.

I have a friend named Ken Smith who has written a wonderful book on managing your time (*It's About Time*, Chosen Books). When I first met Ken, I thought he was an attorney who had gone nuts. He'd left a good practice to give seminars and counsel people on the biblical principles of time and financial management. He went to bed every night at 8:00 p.m. He got up at 4:00 a.m. The schedule for every hour of his day was laid out on a sheet of paper in meticulous fashion. Though very different from him, I learned by following some of his methods to better organize and value my time.

The older I get, the more I realize that if we don't learn to control our time, then we lose control of our lives. Paul said it this way in Ephesians 5:16,17:

> Use every chance you have for doing good, because these are evil times. So do not be foolish but learn what the Lord wants you to do.

Time is a non-renewable resource. Today's opportunities are tomorrow's memories. The consequences of lost opportunities can be eternal. There's the connection to your destiny.

The Number One Quality of a Leader

For over a year, I enjoyed the privilege of working directly with Loren Cunningham, the founder and president of Youth With A Mission. I once heard Loren make a statement on leadership that made a deep and lasting impression on me. He said, "The number one quality of a leader is self-control."

For a while I questioned that concept. What about faith? What about love? Why single out the characteristic of self-control as number one?

The answer related to the nature of leadership. A leader, by definition, "goes before" as a guide for others through example and personal conduct. He's the model that others are to conform to. If he's a good role model, then people feel safe and protected under his leadership. But if he fails in his personal life, he brings others down with him.

The governing quality of a leader's life must be

self-control. As Baptist minister Gordon Hanstad puts it, "The greatest gift I can give to my people is the gift of my own personal holiness."

Think about it. Then think again about all the people in positions of leadership in our nation who are not exercising self-control. Think about the political sex scandals, fallen evangelists, professional athletes with AIDS, and entertainers on drugs, and you will understand why we are where we are.

But we don't have to stay there. Whether you're a leader or not, God wants you to steer the course of your life. He wants you to commit yourself to right and holy living. Jesus has led the way. He's made the power of the Holy Spirit available to all who would follow in His steps. Why not pray this prayer now:

Heavenly Father, I want to live a pure and holy life. I want to turn away from a lifestyle that is uncontrolled. I choose to possess the quality of self-control in the very center of my being.

Help me control my speech. Show me how to order my conduct and time.

Lord, help me to set a good example for all of those who are watching and being influenced by my life. Help me to add to my goodness and knowledge the precious quality of self-control.

Thank you, Father, for hearing and answering my prayer, in the Name of your beloved Son, the Lord Jesus. Amen.

For Thought, Discussion and Action

1. Define self-control. Can you think of any Bible verses that back up your definition?

2. Why is self-control absolutely essential in free societies? If people don't exercise self-control (the other term is self-government), what kind of government will God give them? Explain.

3. What are the three areas of self-control on which we should concentrate? In which ones are you weak? Discuss how you can become strong.

4. Determine to make self-control a guiding quality of your life. Practice it before God, and also in all your human relationships.

9

Endure

When I lived in Washington, D.C., I rubbed shoulders with a Christian leader who was a main spokesman for moral renewal in our country.

Jerry Falwell, pastor of Thomas Road Baptist Church in Lynchburg, Virginia, catapulted into national prominence through the founding of the Moral Majority in the mid-1970s. He struck a chord in the nation's conscience with a call to a return to traditional moral values and a reliance upon God.

For a number of years, he was probably the most loved and hated man in America. Personally, I found him to be humble, sincere, articulate, and deeply committed. We didn't agree on everything. But on the essentials for rebuilding our culture, our hearts were certainly linked together.

One evening he spoke at a rally in an elegant Washington hotel. I don't remember the details of his speech, but I'll always remember one line from it. He said, "The true greatness of an individual is always proportionate to his willingness to *endure testing.*"

At that time, Jerry Falwell was being attacked and maligned by the American press and political left. He passed his test by living out the character quality of perseverance by patiently standing firm in battle in the public arena.

Every great man has to pass the same test. So do *all* followers of the Lord Jesus. For perseverance is not just a mark of greatness. It's the fifth pillar of Christian character found in II Peter 1:6: "and to self-control, [add] *perseverance*" (italics mine).

Live by Your Will—Not by Your Emotions

At first, I had a hard time understanding the difference between self-control and perseverance. Didn't both involve the will? Isn't each a disciplined choice?

Both involve a choice, but they have different meanings. Self-control has to do with restraint exercised over one's impulses. Perseverance involves remaining steadfast despite opposition. Many times, perseverance means that you must be willing to wait. It means not acting hastily or impetuously.

Perseverance is honed through determination and discipline—attributes forged during the hard, battle-weary moments of our lives when we encounter life's harshest tests.

These tests can be physical or mental, and include the gamut of human experience, such as:

- broken relationships, friendships, divorce
- accusation, persecution, and outright slander
- broken health, bodily pain, and suffering
- physical limitations and handicaps
- prejudice and bigotry; cruelty and injustice
- loss of a loved one, a job, or a dream
- loneliness, depression, lack of self-esteem
- lacking a sense of destiny and purpose

When painful circumstances such as these come upon us, we are faced with a choice to hold on and endure, or to give in to our feelings and emotions.

Most of us would rather go along with our feelings. If we feel like going to a movie, we go. If we feel like eating something, we do (whether we're on a diet or not). If we feel like taking a nap, we put off that job around the house.

When we become believers, we bring the habit of living by our feelings into our new life in Christ. If we don't feel like praying, we don't. When we don't feel like going to church, we don't. If we don't feel like going out in evangelism, we find an excuse.

Emotions are a wonderful part of our God-given personality, but they were never designed to be the guiding force in our lives. The "engine" of our lives was always meant to be our will.

I believe that God starts his "endurance training" in the area of the physical. Once we learn to persevere in bodily disciplines, we can apply the same lessons to the spiritual and mental realm.

Let's look at three physical areas where perseverance can be learned. The first one we can thank Adam and Eve for.

Work

Most people need to work to survive. The need to work forces us to set alarm clocks, pull ourselves out of bed when we're still tired, battle traffic or nature, and deal with diverse personalities and circumstances.

By eating the forbidden fruit, Adam and Eve passed on to all their descendants both the curse and the blessing of work. In Genesis 3:17-19, God said:

> So I will put a curse on the ground, and you will have to work very hard for your food. In pain you will eat its food all the days of your life....You will sweat and word hard for your food. Later you will return to the ground.

Hard work, including sweat and pain, is a result of God's cursing the ground following the original sin of mankind. But like most judgments, the pain and labor of work contain a gracious silver lining: by learning to work hard, man develops patience and endurance. This quality of perseverance is both a restraint on sin (can you imagine how much evil would be in the world if people didn't have to work every day?) and a builder of character.

A case in point is the courageous example of my own father. My dad, Dr. Robert Boehme, grew up in the 1930s during the Depression. His father, Herman, worked two eight-hour shifts each day in the rubber factories of Ohio to put food on the table for a family of eight. For as far back as he can remember, my dad wanted to become a doctor. But he wondered how he could ever afford to go to medical school. Also, as the eldest son, he knew that his family needed his help just for survival.

Dad's only answer was to embrace a discipline of hard work. For a number of years, he worked in a rubber factory all night, went to college during the morning, studied all afternoon, slept for two hours, then went back to work again.

Dad did this five days a week for six long years. He eventually graduated with honors, became a family physician, and built up one of the largest medical practices in the state of Washington.

I learned perseverance from his example. One year, he and I sheetrocked my new home together just six weeks after he had open-heart bypass surgery. He never stopped moving. After a ten-minute lunch break, he'd rise to his feet and say, "It's time to get going." Crankily, I would gulp down my remaining bites and try to keep up with this "hard-working German."

One day while we were working, he cut his leg very deeply with a saw. I tried to no avail to persuade him to go to the emergency room. He wouldn't even listen to my pleas. After a brief shouting match between us, he managed to stop the bleeding by wrapping duct tape around his thigh. (What could I say? He was the doctor.) He simply said, "There's no time to stop." When he went home that night, he sewed himself up in his bathroom.

Fasting

Another physical area of our lives where perseverance can be learned is in the area of eating, or more accurately, in the area of not eating—fasting. Forgoing eating for the purpose of prayer and study of God's Word teaches us to persevere against the natural desires of the body.

Jesus began His own earthly ministry with a 40-day fast that rooted His character in perseverance. The Father knew that three years later, He would desperately need this trait to face the agonizing moments of betrayal, flogging, crucifixion, and death. He had already learned endurance in the work world of the carpenter's shop. His final test prior to the launching of His public ministry was to be over the enticement of hunger.

He passed the test. Immediately afterward, He returned to Galilee to preach the Gospel, heal the sick, and proclaim the Kingdom of God (Matthew 4:23). In the Sermon on the Mount, He encouraged His disciples to fast also. "Your Father," He said, "will reward you" (Matthew 6:16-18).

Our body naturally craves food. It doesn't always need it. When we give up eating in order to spend special time with God, we learn to endure the pain of a gnawing stomach for a greater reward.

I remember my first attempts at fasting during my teenage years. I felt as if I were going to die after missing a few meals! My teenage appetite (which had never left a table unsatisfied) had grown to dominate my will. Only the discipline of fasting could break the power of indulgence.

One time, I went on a ten-day fast. After three days, everything in our house began to smell like food. I was weak. Water tasted horrible. I persevered. By the end of the ten days, I had learned some valuable lessons. Since then, I've made weekly and yearly fasts a part of my life.

I would urge you to let fasting become a part of your character development. It's a quality you need to develop for greater challenges that may lie ahead.

Exercise

Another place where endurance can be learned is in the area of physical exercise. It's often a contest of mind over matter. In this case, the "matter" is our finite, human bodies.

Physical exercise has always been an important part of my life. Growing up, I enjoyed many sports (especially football and basketball), and in each one I learned the value of discipline and training.

Paul's words in I Corinthians 9:24-27 stand out:

> You know that in a race all the runners run, but only one gets the prize. So run to win! All those who compete in the games use self-control so they can win a crown. That crown is an earthly thing that lasts only a short time, but our crown will never be destroyed. So I do not run without a goal. I fight like a boxer who is hitting something—not just the air. I treat my body hard and make it my slave so that I myself will not be disqualified after I have preached to others.

Here Paul specifically uses the example of sports training to highlight the importance of perseverance. In sports, we learn to treat our bodies hard, to run to win. If athletes discipline themselves for earthly "medals," then we should certainly do the same for eternal rewards.

One day, while jogging around Sebago Lake in southern Maine, I felt that God wanted to speak to me about the importance of learning perseverance through physical conditioning. I hadn't run for awhile. My legs seemed like lead. In a matter of minutes, I was huffing and puffing. I didn't know if I could go on.

The pain of my out-of-shape body brought back vivid memories of past sports contests. I remembered running wind sprints during tryouts for basketball until the skin hung off the bottom of my blistered feet. I'd persevered then.

I recalled being beat up in football, only to push my aching bones up the field one more time. Once my legs were so sore that I couldn't lift them out of bed. I rolled onto the floor and crawled to the shower. Soon I was back on the field.

If I did it then, I can do it now, I mumbled to myself as I trudged around the lake. No matter how much it hurt, I was determined to keep going. My body kept screaming, "No!" My persevering spirit proclaimed, "Yes!" As I rounded the last corner and stumbled over an imaginary finish line, I thought I heard the Lord saying: "Very good. Now do the same in prayer."

The words cut deep. I'd learned to run to win. But this was just a training ground for the greater issues and duties of life and ministry. What God really wanted to teach me was to persevere in the greater tests of life.

Perfect and Complete

After we have learned endurance through the disciplines of hard work, fasting, and bodily exercise, we can apply this quality to every area of our life. God gives us a phenomenal promise related to perseverance. Here are His words:

> My brothers and sisters, when you have many kinds of troubles, you should be full of joy, because you know that these troubles test your faith, and this will give you persever-

ance. Let your perseverance show itself perfectly in what you do. Then you will be *perfect
and complete and will have everything you need*
(James 1:2-4, italics mine).

God promises we will have problems. He tells us,
though, to rejoice over them, because this testing of
our faith will produce perseverance. And what will
perseverance make us?

"Perfect and complete and will have everything
you need." That means *invincible* to the attack of the
enemy, and thoroughly able to do God's will.

For Thought, Discussion, and Action

1. What is the difference between self-control and
   perseverance? How does God develop the quality of endurance in our lives? What Scriptures
   back this up?

2. What three physical disciplines help us learn to
   endure? Share any experiences you've had in
   learning perseverance in these areas.

3. Why does developing the quality of perseverance
   make us invincible? What people in the Bible
   practiced endurance in accomplishing great ex-
   ploits for God? Explain.

4. If you don't already, begin this week to regularly
   fast and exercise. Start small and develop endurance. Let it continue to grow to greatness.

10

Spend Time with God

The primary goal of our lives should be to become Christlike, or as Peter states in II Peter 1:4, to "share in being like God." There is no greater goal for life—nothing else more worthy of living and dying for.

We've already seen in the first chapter of II Peter four qualities that are essential for achieving our God-given destinies. They are goodness, knowledge, self-control, and perseverance. God possesses all of these traits in infinite proportions. As believers, He comes to live inside of us, and to build these aspects of His character into the very fiber of our spiritual being.

Quality number five brings all of these together. In II Peter 1:6, Peter encourages us, "and to perseverance, [add] godliness."

Godliness is our goal. This brings to mind such things as love, joy, peace, patience, kindness, gentleness, humility, truthfulness, and justice.

In this chapter, we will not focus primarily on what godliness is; rather, we will look at how one becomes a godly person.

Spend Time with God

There is really only one way to become godly. *Godliness comes from spending time with the one who is God.* It's based on the principle that we take on the characteristics of those we spend time with. The writer of the Proverbs said it this way: "Spend time with the wise and you will become wise, but the friends of fools will suffer" (Proverbs 13:20).

This mentions one way of spending time with God: being in the presence of wise people who know and love Him. Here's where Christian fellowship and interaction come in. Being with others in whom Christ dwells allows us to literally be with Him. That's a good reason all by itself to "meet together and encourage each other" (Hebrews 10:25).

But there are two other important ways of spending time with God. I am more convinced all the time that these two disciplines are the greatest things that I can do to be the person God wants me to be.

Be a Lover of Prayer

Prayer is talking to God and letting Him speak back to us. As good communication is a key to any human relationship, so it is vital to our most important relationship: the one with our Creator and Savior. The more we talk with one another, the more comfortable we feel in each other's presence.

Marriage taught me this. I'm quiet by nature; my wife Shirley is talkative. Many evenings she's had to practically pry the details of my day out of me as I buried my head behind a newspaper. Often, just as I've been dozing off, she has drawn from my inner being the thoughts of my heart.

She was right. We need to talk about every aspect of our lives. That's how we've learned to love each other more, respect our differences, share our joys and hurts, and develop the comfort of intimacy.

It's the same in our relationship with God. I've never met a man or woman committed to regular prayer who did not have an intimate relationship with the Father. The two go hand in hand. But I've met many people who feel that God is distant. They also admit that they rarely talk to Him.

In spending time with God in prayer, I would like to make three practical suggestions. Paul said in I Thessalonians 5:17 to "pray continually." That means to do it all the time. Always be talking to God. On your jog, in the shower (you can sing songs there, too!), during your trip to work or school, at your desk, over the dishes, while mowing the lawn, while talking to a client, lying in bed, on a trip, at the dentist (pray like mad), or any place you go. Brother Lawrence, the famous dishwasher monk, called it "practicing the presence of God." It's being aware that God is always there.

Second, it's important to have a special place for private prayer. Mark 1:35 says that Jesus "went to a lonely place, where he prayed." Seclusion is necessary for developing intimacy. In a quiet place, away from other distractions, deeper and more intimate conversations can take place.

Jesus had the hills of Galilee and the Garden of Gethsemane. Daniel had his room. Moses had the tabernacle. Solomon had a temple. Habakkuk, a tower. Peter, a rooftop. In my own life, no matter where we've lived, I've always found special places where I could be alone with God. In one area, it was a secluded beach. While in Washington, D.C., I oftentimes went to the quiet western steps of the U.S. Capitol. Now I use an office in our home.

Third, you need to schedule regular, daily prayer times with your heavenly Father. Prayer needs to be spontaneous, but also one of the most stable habits of our lives. All the godly men and women of the Bible prayed frequently and everywhere.

Do you know which time of day most of them chose for a regular prayer time? The morning. Notice the full quotation of Mark 1:35: "Early the next morning, while it was still dark, Jesus woke and left the house. He went to a lonely place, where he prayed."

You'll find this pattern throughout Scripture. It's good to establish a habit of early morning prayer. Then you'll have the spiritual strength to pray while on the run the rest of the day.

But there's a better way still. The Bible actually teaches that the very best habit of prayer is three times a day. Daniel prayed three times daily in his upstairs room in Babylon (Daniel 6:10). David said, "Morning, noon, and night I am troubled and upset, but he will listen to me" (Psalm 55:17). In the same way that most of us try to eat three meals a day, the Bible says that through prayer we can have three "spiritual feasts" throughout the day.

In my own life, I first established the morning quiet time, then a time of prayer at the end of the day, and later began to snatch some time with God during my lunch break. The result was tremendous.

But there is another way to have quality communication with our Father.

Be a Lover of the Bible

The Bible is the greatest book of all time. It is God's love letter to each of us. It has sold more copies and been produced in more languages than any other piece of literature in history. Getting His message out to a sinful world cost God thousands of lives (people martyred for their faith).

As a book, the Bible is unique. It is the only pure and unadulterated written source of truth in all the world. Its central message is God's redeeming love through the death and resurrection of Jesus Christ. If prayer is our way of communicating with God, then the Bible is God's way of communicating with us. It is alive and living, sharper than a double-edged sword (Hebrews 4:12).

There are a number of different ways that the Bible can be used for personal spiritual growth. Let's take a look at three of them.

Meditation

We should meditate daily on God's word. Psalm 1 promises that all who meditate on the Bible will be strong, like a tree planted by a river (Psalm 1:3). Joshua 1:8 tells us if we study His teachings, then "you will be wise and successful in everything."

Bible meditation is thinking deeply and often about truths in the Scripture. Memorization can be helpful, but it is not synonymous with meditating. Bible meditation is taking a verse or phrase from God's word and contemplatively "chewing it over" in your mind to extract the nutrition. Its literal meaning is "to muse or mutter."

I enjoy taking a verse out of my devotional reading and thinking about it for the rest of the day. David said it this way, "How I love your teachings! I think about them all day long" (Psalm 119:97).

Bible Study

Another way of spending time with God in His word is regular Bible study. Studying the Bible, as opposed to meditating on a few verses, involves a more in-depth and thorough approach to a subject. It could be the analysis of a major theme or teaching, using a concordance or other helps to gain a wide breadth of knowledge, or the study of a particular person or character quality in Scripture. Usually it involves hours and/or days of exploration.

I've tried to make Bible study an ongoing part of my life. Once I studied the theme of salvation in every book of the New Testament. A few years ago, I did research on the quality of servanthood. A Christian never stops being a student. David said it best when he stated, "I think about your orders and study your ways" (Psalm 119:15).

Devotions

A final method of being with God in His word is having daily, total Bible devotions. This is the habit of reading four or five chapters of God's word every day to wash and refresh your soul. It's different from meditation. There usually isn't time for study, either. Reading the Bible devotionally requires taking 20 to 30 minutes a day (usually in combination with a prayer time) to simply let God's word "shower" you with truth. Billy Graham once said that reading four or five chapters in the Bible each day was one of the most important habits in his life.

And what's crucial is the total reading of Scripture from cover to cover. God inspired the whole Bible. Most wrong doctrine and incomplete teaching come from lifting individual Scriptures and ideas out of the full context of the Bible.

Unfortunately, many people read the Bible like it's a smorgasbord: they pick and choose at random. When they want encouragement, they read Psalms. Normally they prefer the New Testament to the Old (even though God made the Old Testament four times as big as the New). When they're depressed, they read Ecclesiastes. When they're in a learning mode, they look at Proverbs. When they're about to get married, they turn to the Song of Solomon.

The problem with this method is that some parts of the Bible never get read. Whole portions of God's word are neglected.

Long ago, a wise man encouraged me to read through the Bible once each year, reading four to five chapters a day, from Genesis through Revelation. I have practiced this habit for twenty years, and consider it one of the most important parts of my life.

Company Determines Character

Who we spend time with determines what we become. Paul said it best in I Corinthians 15:33 that "Bad company corrupts good character" (NIV). The opposite is also true: "Good company produces good character." There is no better company than God Himself.

In the last chapter, we saw the importance of disciplined perseverance. Notice now what Paul points to as the most important area of our lives to live by determination and discipline:

But do not follow foolish stories that disagree with God's truth, but *train yourself to serve God.* Training your body helps you in some ways, but serving God helps you in every way *by bringing you blessings in this life and in the future life, too* (I Timothy 4:7,8, italics mine).

The greatest disciplines of our lives should not be in the areas of work, fasting, exercise, or any other physical activity. Our greatest persevering commitment must be to attain godliness.

Godliness holds the promise for this life and the one to come. *It is a master key to your destiny,* both here on earth and also in heaven.

For Thought, Discussion, and Action

1. List as many attributes of God as you can think of. Which ones do you have the greatest need of developing right now in your own life?

2. There are three ways to spend time with God. What is the third way that we only briefly mentioned? Can you list some people whom it would be wise for you to spend time with? How can you arrange to do it?

3. What is the weakest part of your prayer life? What's the neediest part of your life in God's word? What can you do this week to strengthen these weaknesses?

4. Get a read-through-the-Bible devotional this week, and begin reading the Scriptures from cover to cover. Establish quiet times as a way of life. Enjoy God and become like Him.

11

Be Kind

For the sixth time, Peter adds an ingredient to his recipe for destiny-bound believers, "and to godliness, [add] *brotherly kindness*" (II Peter 1:7, italics mine).

The final two character qualities for fulfilling God's calling on our lives are like icing on the cake. They're beautiful, tender attributes that round out the spectrum of Christlikeness.

At this point, some of you may be thinking: *I can't make it! All this character stuff requires Herculean will-power. Goodness. Knowledge. Self-Control. Perseverance. Godliness....Woe is me, for I am undone (or at least overwhelmed).*

Well, be encouraged! Although we're all tainted by sin, all of us are also recipients of God's grace, and in need of His power. God does not ask us to grit our teeth and climb the spiritual Himalayas on our own. Rather, "He has given us everything we need to live and to serve God....Because you have these blessings, *do your best to add these things to your lives*" (II Peter 1:3,5, italics mine).

In this chapter, we'll look at *kindness*. Peter describes it as "brotherly kindness."

A Kinder, Gentler You and Me

Kindness is something we learn best by spending time with God. God lives to bless and encourage. He is a giver at heart. He spends much time sprinkling the world with dewdrops of kindness in the form of the provision of food, the healing of sickness, the grace of forgiveness, the joy of relationship, and the rescues from danger, calamity, sin, and despair.

The Old Testament proclaims, "I have seen you in the Temple and have seen your strength and glory. Because your love is better than life, I will praise you" (Psalm 63:2,3). The New Testament adds its agreement, "People hated us, and we hated each other. But when the kindness and love of God our Savior was shown, he saved us because of his mercy" (Titus 3:3,4).

God desires us to be kind like He is. Kindness is doing those little things that will bless and encourage someone else. Kindness is the warmth of a smile. Kindness is the comfort of a hug. It's the thoughtfulness of a gift, the uplifting of a compliment. God wants the world to see a kinder and gentler people.

Creative Acts of Blessing

Because being kind is doing little things for someone else, most acts of kindness don't require much money. They only need to be thoughtful, creative, and timely.

During basketball season my senior year in high school, I had a "secret angel" (a very kind girl) assigned to me. On game days, I would find crepe-paper streamers, balloons, or encouraging notes of support at my locker. Sometimes I would find my favorite candy bars. At the end of the season, I received a scrapbook of my accomplishments.

Those little kindnesses made me feel ten feet tall! They built me up. They made me soar (a little like Michael Jordan). They blessed and enriched my spirit. And none required much material wealth.

In my early days with Youth With A Mission in Europe, I experienced even greater expressions of kindness among brothers and sisters in Christ. While studying together at a Bavarian castle in southern Germany, I watched scores of young people grow in their appreciation of the kindness of God and begin to express it in concrete ways toward one another. Sometimes it was a Scripture verse placed on a pillow. Or a surprise payment on a tuition bill.

Each week, we had a "love feast." These feasts were patterned after the love feasts mentioned in Jude 12, where meals were shared by the early church in an atmosphere of joy and caring. In the 18th Century, the Moravians practiced this custom, and when John Wesley attended a love feast, he said it was like visiting heaven on earth. Youth With A Mission still holds love feasts at many locations around the world. At our German love feasts, the tables were decorated and the program was built around fellowship and encouragement. Expressions of kindness inflated our sense of family and individual worth. Everyone was made to feel special.

With all the brokenness and low self-esteem in the world, it's time for an explosion of kindness.

Good, Appropriate Manners

A small, but significant, way to manifest kindness is in the use of good manners in relating to different groups of people. In our society, we're told that everyone is equal, which is often interpreted to mean that no one is special. Another viewpoint is that our value is based on our abilities, positions, appearance, or other criteria.

However, the Bible teaches that all human beings are equal in value, but we're not equal in our gifts, positions, or functions in life. This doesn't mean that any one of us is of greater value, but merely that each of us is unique. We should honor the unique attributes God has given to each person.

Good manners reveal our recognition of God-given distinctions among individuals. Let's look at three situations where good manners are called for.

First, we must show appropriate manners toward those in authority (I Peter 2:13-17). Leadership is a God-ordained function (Romans 13:1). When we do not show honor to congressmen, presidents, policemen, soldiers, and others in positions of authority, we pull down our society. Sarcasm, political cartoons, and outright disrespect shatter self-worth.

I'll never forget a conversation I once had with an American soldier at an airport. When I thanked him for serving in the army to defend our freedom, his jaw dropped. Tears filled his eyes and he said, "Thank you so much for your encouragement. No one has ever thanked me before for serving my country. I didn't think anyone cared."

Second, we need to be sensitive toward the elderly. The Bible teaches that the aged should be shown special honor (I Timothy 5:1,2). Today we often do the reverse. We make fun of our forgetful relatives. We stick our parents and grandparents in nursing homes and convalescent centers. We glamorize youth.

I have greatly enjoyed special relationships with many elderly relatives and friends. One such friend, Mrs. Ann Malone, was 95 years old when we first met (she lived to be 103). I often went to her home to have tea, then "allowed" her to serve me her homemade apple pie. Her eyes would sparkle when I asked for a second piece. Sometimes we listened to her "talking books" together, and I always asked her to tell me a story about her childhood growing up in a sod house in Nebraska. If we stop to listen to our elders, we can learn a lot.

Third, we must display special manners toward members of the opposite sex. The unisex revolution left millions of men and women confused. The drive for basic equal rights has been good. But the pushing of equal roles and responsibilities has broken up

many homes and led to the horrible rise of lesbian-
ism and homosexuality in the Western world.

I believe that God created men and women with
different strengths. Women are generally superior to
men in areas such as feeling, intuition, physical
beauty, and social graces. Men are generally better
in mental logic, physical strength, and the vision of
leadership. These are not stereotypes, but rather de-
scriptions of the unique gifts God created in us.

We should celebrate these distinctions. When my
wife hands me a jar that needs opening, or asks my
opinion on something, I'm delighted to help her.
When I open the car door for her, or listen to her
insight on matters, she recognizes that I respect her
and need her perspective.

Ask God to show you the special differences that
He sees in people, then honor those differences with
acts of kindness.

Quick, Wholehearted Forgiveness

The greatest act of kindness that can be offered to
a person is the gift of forgiveness. Think back to your
own salvation experience when the "kindness and
love of God" (Titus 3:4) was shown to you. Weights
dropped off your shoulders.

No moment will ever be as important to you as
the moment you experience the forgiveness of sins.
The greatest evidence of God's kindness toward us
is that He has chosen to be forgiving toward the
undeserving and unworthy.

We celebrate His grace. We should pass it on to
others. Paul admonished the Ephesian church:

Do not be bitter or angry or mad. Never
shout angrily or say things to hurt others.
Never do anything evil. Be kind and loving to
each other, and forgive each other just as God
forgave you in Christ (Ephesians 4:31).

I'll never forget the forgiveness that a friend

named Steve Hulst offered me during the summer of 1976. Shirley (who was my fiancee at that time) and I had worked all week at a large YWAM festival near Philadelphia. Our mobile office during the area-wide Jesus Rally was a small trailer that Steve had loaned us for a few days.

While driving back to New Jersey the evening after the event finished, I gasped in horror as I watched through my rear view mirror as the trailer separated from the hitch. With sparks flying, the trailer careened out of sight, did a 180-degree turn, and smashed onto its side.

By the time I got to it, it lay totaled on the highway. A sickening hiss rose from the smashed propane tanks that lay buried underneath it. In horror, I remembered that the trailer wasn't insured. My heart pounded as I thought about telling Steve.

With the help of some people who had stopped to view the accident, we miraculously flipped the trailer over onto its wheels and eased it down the road to Hammonton.

Arriving at the YWAM center in the early hours of the morning, I crawled into bed and dreaded the arrival of daylight. I knew I would have to face Steve. I kept trying to figure out a way I could pay for the damage.

I found Steve in his office around 9:00 a.m., and got straight to the point.

"Steve," I practically whispered, "I've got something to tell you. I'm so sorry, but I wrecked your trailer last night." I blurted out the painful details. I braced myself for his outcry. It seemed forever in coming.

Without blinking an eye, Steve responded, "Oh, that's okay. It's only a trailer. Are you okay?"

His forgiving words seemed to lift a thousand-pound weight off my back! His arm over my shoulder, we walked outside to view the wreckage. He refused to let me try to pay for the damage. Grace had rescued my day of dread.

A Trillion Points of Kindness

The more we get to know God, the more we will understand "the very great riches of his grace by being kind to us in Christ Jesus" (Ephesians 2:7). God is infinitely kind to His creation. His greatest act of kindness was the gift of His Son for our sins.

And God wants us to be like Him. He wants us to demonstrate a trillion points of kindness by glorifying the unique differences in people that can be encouraged through simple acts, thoughtful manners, and forgiveness.

And yet there is still another character trait (as the apostle Paul says, "a more excellent way") that will propel you toward your God-appointed destiny. It happens to be the greatest one of all.

For Thought, Discussion, and Action

1. What is the main way we learn to be kind? (Hint: refer to Chapter 10.) Think of ways that God has been kind to you.

2. What are the three primary ways that we can show kindness to one another? Share a meaningful story from your own life of how another person was kind to you in one of these ways.

3. How do good manners show our recognition of God-given differences among people? Explain. In what ways can you improve your manners (acts of kindness) toward the opposite sex? Toward those in authority? Toward the elderly?

4. Make a list of people that God would have you creatively bless. Begin today to let God's kindness shine through you.

12

Love is All

Love is the summation of all the character traits that Peter encouraged us to develop in our lives. John told us that "God is love" (I John 4:8). Jesus also told us that love is the most important quality of a believer: "All people will know that you are my followers if you love each other" (John 13:35).

Wanted: True Love

The world understands little about the nature of love. For some people, it is equated with sexual desire and lust. For others, it is a mood that you can fall in or out of. The reason for this confusion is that we've separated the definition of love from its author and greatest expression, Jesus Christ.

True love—what the Bible calls *agape* love—is a choice that comes from the heart, based on purity of motive and rightness of knowledge. It can be summed up like this: <u>Love is choosing to do what is best for another person from God's perspective.</u>

Sometimes love is accompanied by strong feelings; other times it is a difficult decision made in the absence of any supportive emotion. But real love always does what's best for another. That's why sexual lust isn't love. It only takes for itself, and hurts others in the process.

One of the best-known Bible verses defines love clearly: "God loved the world so much that he gave his one and only Son so that whoever believes in him may not be lost, but have eternal life" (John 3:16).

God loved the world so much that He sent His son to live and die for others. In this chapter, we will look at three different expressions of love viewed in the life of the Lord Jesus.

Love is Choosing to be Gentle and Compassionate

I have heard it said that the six-word autobiography of Jesus Christ is found in Mark 8:2, where Jesus said, "I have compassion on the multitudes" (NKJV).

When faced with the needs of the people in Palestine, Jesus showed mercy and compassion. He healed the sick. He encouraged the distressed. He fed the poor. He opened the eyes of the blind.

Love shows itself in gentle acts toward those in pain. Whether his efforts are directed toward a child with a skinned knee, a person without food, or a friend who is distraught, the loving person attempts to alleviate suffering.

A few weeks ago, while I was doing some street evangelism with two young people in a needy area of Seattle, we came upon a man slumped on a dirty bench at a bus stop. It was obvious that he was cold and hungry. One of the young people immediately ran back to our meeting place for a supply of sandwiches. Tears came to the man's eyes as we served him and talked and prayed about his future. This was an example of compassionate love.

But love does not always show itself in kind and compassionate actions. Contrary to Sunday school myth, "gentle Jesus, meek and mild" is an incomplete picture of our Savior. Sometimes Jesus' love took a different form.

Love is Choosing to be Strong and Angry

We know the story of Jesus and the money changers in the temple (one account of the action is found in John 2:14-16). When Jesus went to the temple in Jerusalem, instead of witnessing prayer and devotion, He saw greed and corruption among those buying and selling cattle, sheep, and doves in and near the house of God. What was His response?

- He made a large whip out of cords with knots in them.

- He flailed it repeatedly to drive away the defilers.

- He crashed over the money tables, sending coins bouncing in all directions.

- In the end, He shouted above the roar, "Take these things out of here! Don't make my Father's house a place for buying and selling!"

A loving response? Jesus' actions were a perfect expression of doing what was best toward those with greedy and hardened hearts. Strong, righteous indignation was called for. This was no less an act of love than the compassion shown to the multitudes.

Another example of "tough love" is found in Matthew 23, where Jesus gets involved in loving the scribes and Pharisees. Let's examine a few of Jesus' loving words from the standpoint of our definition of love (doing what is best for another):

Woe to you, teachers of the law and Pharisees, you hypocrites! You shut the kingdom of heaven in men's faces. You yourselves do not enter, nor will you let those enter who are trying to.

You blind guides! You strain out a gnat but swallow a camel.

You clean the outside of the cup and dish, but inside they are full of greed and self-indulgence. Blind Pharisee! First clean the inside of the cup and dish, and then the outside also will be clean.

You snakes! You brood of vipers! How will you escape being condemned to hell? (Matthew 23:13,14,24-26,33 NIV).

Most of us don't associate these words with love! That's because we think that being "loving" means being gentle, warm, and fuzzy. But everything Jesus did was a manifestation of the love of God.

We need to understand that even earthly judgment is a loving act of God. It is designed to bring people to repentance and saving faith. As C.S. Lewis pointed out, judgment is simply a severe form of mercy (love).

As parents, my wife and I know well this aspect of love. Many times we have wept with righteous anger as we spanked a disobedient child. We love them enough to do what's best for them. It would be easy not to discipline them, but it would not be loving.

Love is Choosing to Give and to Sacrifice

Another aspect of love is the willingness to sacrificially give of yourself for the benefit of another person. Again, we see an example of this in the life of the Lord Jesus.

Paul tells us in Philippians 2:5-8:

In your lives you must think and act like Christ Jesus. Christ himself was like God in everything. But he did not think that being equal with God was something to be used for his own benefit. But he gave up his place with God and made himself nothing. He was born to be a man and became like a servant. And when he was living as a man, he humbled himself and was fully obedient to God, even when that caused his death—death on a cross.

The final act of Jesus' love mission to the world was to lay down His life for us. He "gave up His place"; He "became like a servant"; He "humbled himself...even when that caused His death."

God loved the world by giving His only son. For 2,000 years, this has defined for us the ultimate act of love. Others have followed Jesus' example. In times of war or crisis, they have "laid down their lives for their friends."

But the benchmark is Jesus.

The Spectrum of Love

As we've seen, love shows itself in many different forms. Love is, really, an action that responds appropriately to the state of the heart it is encountering. If the heart is broken and tender, love can take gentle forms. If the heart is hardened, strong measures are called for.

Listed below are a few examples of Jesus' loving responses to different "states of heart" (people) that He encountered in His ministry:

Encounter	State of Heart	Loving Action
Adulterous woman	Repentant	Forgiveness
Woman at the well	Open, curious	Friendly
Rich young rule	Hedging	Exhortation
Angry disciples	Upset	Gentle rebuke
Pharisees	Religious hypocrisy	Angry rebuke

Love is the ultimate mark of the Christian (John 13:35). None of us can fully love another person without the empowering of the Holy Spirit. The manner in which we display love is an indication of how far we've come toward our goal of being more like God.

Character for Eternity

We have looked at seven character qualities that will enable us to fulfill our destiny. Let it be firmly established in your mind that your calling will be determined to a large extent by your character.

A few years ago, after speaking on this subject to a group in Texas, I noticed a young girl waiting her turn to chat with me near the podium. She approached me, looked me in the eye, and said very quietly, "You've given us your best, haven't you?"

Her remark stunned me. Was this teaching on good character the most exciting, most eloquent, most electrifying speech that she had ever heard? Had I just delivered my most moving sermon ever? I certainly didn't think so.

Then it dawned on me what she meant. I nodded and replied, "Yes, you're right. I've just told you the best advice I can give to help you lead a godly and fruitful life. I've given you my best."

To summarize, each of us must heed Peter's advice. We must:

Be good with a pure heart;

Grow in knowledge by becoming strong in spirit;

Control ourselves in all areas;

Persevere when times are tough;

Be godly by spending time with Him;

Be kind as God is to all; and

Live a life of love through the grace of Jesus.

If you do these things, God promises you in His word that you will never fall, you will be useful and productive, and you will receive a rich welcome into heaven.

Character is destiny. Strive to master and achieve it, and your life's calling will open up before you.

For Thought, Discussion, and Action

1. What is your definition of love? How does the world define love? Discuss why love is "doing what's best for another from God's perspective."

2. What expressions of love are missing from our world today? Share some examples from your own life of times when people really loved you. What form did their love take?

3. Why is love the "mark" of a Christian? Why can't the devil counterfeit the character quality of true love?

4. Think of people you know who have different states of heart. How should you love them? Determine to do it by God's grace.

Section III

You Have a Destiny—Receive It

I have glorified you on the earth. I have finished the work which you have given me to do (John 17:4 NIV).

We have around us many people whose lives tell us what faith means. So let us run the race that is before us and never give up. We should remove from our lives anything that would get in the way and the sin that so easily holds us back. Let us look only to Jesus, the One who began our faith and who makes it perfect. He suffered death on the cross. But he accepted the shame as if it were nothing because of the joy that God put before him. And now he is sitting at the right side of God's throne (Hebrews 12:1,2).

God wants us to know why He brought us into this world. In this section, we will look at how we *receive* God's vision for our lives, and walk it out through the normal challenges of life. Others who have gone before us can show us the way. The Lord Jesus Himself is the best example of a man who lived out His destiny in perfect detail.

Many things can hinder God's plans for our lives. We need to understand ourselves so that we can develop the gifts He's entrusted to us. There are detours that many of us take by straying from His pathway.

But there's hope when that happens. He is the God who restores. A creative potential still lies ahead. We simply need to get back on track, seek Him with all our heart, and *receive* the exciting destiny that He longs for us to fulfill.

13

God's Hall of Fame

One of my dad's most cherished childhood memories was strolling hand in hand with his father through the stately corridors of Pro Football's Hall of Fame in Canton, Ohio. He was able to see first-hand the jerseys, helmets, shoes, footballs, and paraphernalia used by his sports idols. Years later, inspired by their achievements, he went on to excel in the game himself. He became an all-state selection during his last year of high school.

Halls of fame remind us of people who were the best at what they did. I'd like to take you to "God's Hall of Fame." Here you'll find the names and accomplishments of ordinary people who were faithful to live out God's plan for their lives.

It's really a Hall of Faith. You could even earn a place in it. Acts 13:36 makes this statement regarding Israel's second king: "David did God's will during his lifetime." If we "trust and obey" Him, we join His great cloud of witnesses (see Hebrews 11).

That's the key. It's obedience that gets you "elected" into these hallowed halls. Let's begin our tour down the first corridor.

Well-Known People of Destiny in the Bible

The Bible is filled with the stories of people who made their mark in history. What made them great was not their unusual gifts or superhuman abilities. Rather, it was obedience to God's direction. Let's look at a few of them:

Abraham. God gave Abram a glimpse of his destiny when He spoke to him in Genesis 12:1-3 (we don't know how he spoke), and promised that he would have a land, become the father of a great nation, and that all people on earth would be blessed through him. Abram was at that time the equivalent of a 30-year-old man (a 75-year-old who lived to be 175). Abraham believed that God had a purpose for his life, and he eventually became the father of the Jewish nation.

An interesting point to note is that over the 100-year span from Abraham's call to his death, the Bible records that God "spoke" to Abraham only four to five times. That's 20 to 25 years between revelations. Abraham was truly a man of faith.

Joseph. At the ripe young age of 17, God gave Joseph two dreams that foretold his life's destiny. The details were sketchy, but the main points were clear: Joseph would be a leader, and would rise to a position of authority over all of his family members.

Soon after this, Joseph experienced the "death of a vision" (more on that in Chapter 15) by being sold into slavery and ending up in prison. But he lived to see God's promise come true.

Moses. His life's destiny was sovereignly preserved from the moment of birth when he was placed in a basket in the Nile River. After growing up in Pharaoh's palace, both Exodus 3:7-10 and Acts 7:22-25 say that Moses had a general sense of being called to be a deliverer of Israel from bondage in Egypt.

But he went about it in the wrong way, and ended up being tested for 40 years in the desert of Midian. That's the death of a vision for an entire generation. He eventually obeyed God, and fulfilled his original calling of deliverance.

David. Can you imagine what must have gone through young David's mind when Samuel anointed him with the oil reserved for crowning kings? There was already a king. David was only a boy. But this was the moment of revelation of God's purpose for his life.

That calling didn't come to pass easily. There were giants to kill, years of being hunted like an animal, and even exile in a foreign land. But after a 15- to 20-year test, "David did God's will during his lifetime."

Jeremiah. He's one of the few in the Bible who can trace his destiny back to before his actual conception. He says in Jeremiah 1:4-7 that "the Lord spoke these words to me: 'Before I made you in your mother's womb, I chose you. Before you were born, I set you apart for a special work. I appointed you as a prophet to the nations.'"

Jeremiah was given a prophetic gift that he would use to shape the destinies of nations over at least a 50-year period. He understood this calling as a boy. That sense of life purpose was an obvious anchor to his incredible ministry, because not once in his book does it ever record that the Jewish people received his words. That's faithfulness in the face of rejection.

John the Baptist. His destiny was heralded by an angel in Luke 1:15-17, and expanded on by his father Zechariah in verses 67-77. Like Jeremiah, he was also called before birth, then prepared in character for 30 years before fulfilling his destiny—being the forerunner of Jesus. His was a ministry that lasted only 9 to 18 months.

Obviously, God's timing is different for each person. Despite the shortness of his life purpose, he is still called by Jesus the greatest man who ever lived (see Matthew 11:11).

Peter. Jesus called this impetuous disciple (with whom we love to identify) to be a leader in the early church (Matthew 16:18). After his denial of the Lord, his destiny came into true fruition (see Acts).

Somewhere along the way, Peter came to understand which group of people he was called to minister to—the Jews (Galatians 2:7). His destiny was to be a pillar in the church, a Jewish evangelist, and, as prophesied, a martyr for his faith (John 21:18).

Paul. Three times in the book of Acts, the apostle Paul gives his testimony. Each time, he mentions the calling of Jesus on the road to Damascus, and the life purpose that grew out of that experience. His destiny included that of being a missionary, and in particular, that of being the apostle to the Gentiles.

Near the end of his life, Paul concluded that God had planned his life before he had been born. In Galatians 1:15,16, he stated with conviction, "But God had special plans for me and set me apart for his work even before I was born. He called me through his grace and showed his son to me so that I might tell the Good News about him to those who are not Jewish."

Each of these eight people had a sense of destiny that sustained them. Each of them heard and obeyed the voice of God.

But there are others not as famous who deserve a place in God's Hall of Fame. Let's turn down another corridor.

Little-Known People of Destiny in the Bible

Our first group of people were giants of the faith. But I'd like to introduce you to some other biblical heroes you may not have heard about. In many ways, these lesser-known greats were as important to history as their famous counterparts. They're just as important to God. But they were called to do different things. (It's good to be introduced to some of these people now; otherwise, it might be somewhat embarrassing to meet them one day in heaven.)

Have you heard of:

Eliezer. He was the manager of Abraham's household. His calling in life was to be a good steward and administrator of Abraham's possessions. He wasn't called to be the father of a nation, but was destined by God to serve the one who was.

Bezalel and Oholiab. Four chapters of the Old Testament are devoted to these obscure servants of God. They were builders of the tabernacle. Moses said that the Lord gave them the skill to cut designs in metal and stone, plan and sew designs in fine linen, and weave great things. They were also given the ability to teach (see Exodus 35:31-35). God destined them to help make His first earthly dwelling. It was a wonderful destiny that others with similar talents share today.

In today's missions movement, God is calling many practically skilled men and women to use their gifts in ways similar to Bezalel and Oholiab. Whether they are contractors, masons, electricians, artists, or interior designers, many gifted people are finding their destiny in God's Kingdom by using their skills for Him, either at home or on the mission field. In YWAM, we call these vital, short-term volunteers *Mission Builders.* They are as essential to God's work worldwide now as they were in the days of Moses.

Hannah. She was given the privilege of being the mother of Samuel, the last judge of Israel. God answered her fervent desire to bear a child with the promise of a son. By raising and releasing him to the service of God, she influenced and benefitted an entire nation. This is one of God's greatest callings: that of godly motherhood.

Ahiezer. Praise God for the destiny of a soldier. He was a leader in David's army—a frontline warrior—who was crucial to the fulfillment of David's destiny. Without him, and others like him, a righteous kingdom could not have been established.

Asaph, Heman, and Jeduthun. These three talented musicians shared God's vision for worship and song. Through His inspiration, they wrote a number of the psalms and guided the young nation in the worship of Jehovah.

Anna. Luke 2:36-38 tells us that she was a prophetess who spent most of her life as an intercessor in the temple. Her faithfulness to this calling of intercessory prayer was rewarded with a glimpse of the Christ child at His dedication.

Mary, Joanna, and Susanna. God's plan for their lives was to provide for the ministry of others. They possessed the gifts of stewardship of money and resources, financial management, and generosity. They were a source of financial support for Jesus and His disciples (Luke 8:2,3).

Tertius. We've all heard of Paul, but few have heard of Tertius. Without him, you might never have heard of Paul. He was Paul's traveling companion and personal secretary. He had the gift of writing, and because of his faithfulness, we enjoy the wonderful epistles that Paul received from God and Tertius penned.

There's a third wing we want to visit before we leave God's Hall of Fame.

People of Destiny in Church History

Since Bible times, many faithful people have gone forth to serve God's Kingdom. In this part of our tour, I will mention several who have influenced my life:

John Hus was burned at the stake for his profession of faith and leadership of the Bohemian Christians during the Middle Ages. His sense of vision and destiny gave birth to the Bohemian Brethren—a revival movement that lasted for over 900 years.

Francis of Assisi was the compassionate monk

who discipled the world in the ways of mercy and relief. He knew his destiny lay among the downtrodden and forsaken. His example has motivated others right up to the present day.

Martin Luther is the man who had the guts to take on a backslidden church and bring reformation. He lived with a sense of purpose, regardless of the risks and despite the cost.

Hudson Taylor was a missionary giant, and his calling to the Chinese people launched an entire movement of missions into the unreached interiors of the world.

Charles Finney was a lawyer who, after being converted, understood his calling to be an "advocate for Christ." His revival ministry touched hundreds of thousands in the United States and abroad.

Billy Graham understood his call to be an evangelist at a very early age, and stayed true to his calling with simplicity and integrity for a fruitful and effective lifetime.

Loren Cunningham, the founder of YWAM, saw his life's purpose in a vision while a teenager, and was faithful to "obey the heavenly vision." Thousands have gone into world evangelism because of Loren's obedience to fulfill the Great Commission.

The names of some of these individuals are in history books; others are recorded only in God's Hall of Fame. Before we end our tour, we need to visit a new wing not yet completed. Over its entryway are these freshly painted words:

People of Destiny—Now and in the Future

This is an awfully big wing. There's room for every person now living or destined by God to be born in the future.

Notice the display that we stand in front of. Isn't that *your* picture hanging on the wall? Do you see the large canvas that awaits the details of your life?

God is waiting for you to begin today to fulfill the destiny He has assigned you. He has promised to provide all the materials and energy you need. All he needs is your faith and obedience.

Our tour failed to visit one other area in God's Hall of Fame. It's so important that it deserves a special building all by itself. It contains the greatest example of a man who fulfilled his destiny. His name is Jesus. He is the Man of Destiny.

For Thought, Discussion, and Action

1. What other people in the Bible are a part of God's Hall of Fame? How were they faithful to fulfill their destiny in life?

2. Do you have to be famous to be a part of God's Hall of Fame (or Faith)? What's the simple criteria? Can you state it in one word?

3. Discuss some modern-day examples of people who are obeying God's plans for their lives. What can you do to imitate them?

4. Decide what your next step of obedience needs to be. Commit yourself to read the biographies of great men and women who have gone before. Follow in their footsteps.

14

Jesus—Man of Destiny

Have you ever wondered what Jesus was like as a boy? Did He argue with His brothers and sisters? Did He cry when He skinned His knee? (Or did He just heal it?) Did He ever "multiply His lunch" when He was extra hungry from working in the carpentry shop?

The Bible tells us only one story about the boyhood of Jesus (found in Luke 2:41-52). When He was 12, He stayed behind in Jerusalem to talk to the religious leaders in the temple. His mother and father were frantic. They looked for Him for three days (that's a long time for anxious parents). Finally, they found Him in the house of God. His matter-of-fact explanation was, "Why were you looking for me? Didn't you know that I must be in my Father's house?" (Luke 2:49).

The message of this story is very simple: Jesus had a sense of destiny at a very early age. As a 12-year-old, He understood that His Heavenly Father had sent Him on a mission. It surprised Him that His parents didn't know that.

Luke tells us that He then spent 18 additional years at home developing character, obeying His parents, growing in wisdom and stature, and growing in favor with God and men.

At the age of 30, He began to live the greatest and most fruitful life that the world was ever to record.

He knew that He had been born for a purpose, and His entire life was consumed with fulfilling it.

Man of Destiny

As Luke records, Jesus was willing to prepare Himself fully for His call and await God's timing for its manifestation.

Jesus is our perfect example in all areas of life. As the God-man, He revealed to us all the aspects of God's character. "Jesus Christ is exactly like him" (Colossians 1:15). When we want to learn about faith, we turn to Him as the most faithful man who ever lived. When we want to know how to live a life of love, we study His words and actions. When we desire to develop servanthood, the best thing we can do is model the life of the servant king who sacrificed everything to bring us to God.

And so it is with the subject of destiny. Jesus is our perfect model of a man with a sense of destiny. In this chapter, we will take a look at the greatest life ever lived.

The Magic of Threes

I remember the old three-legged lunch stools that I sat on in the school cafeteria when I was growing up. With three different supports, I could always find a way to balance them. Two legs would have been useless; a stool with four legs usually wobbled. But with three supports, I had stability and control.

We have a three-legged ladder at home. It's made especially for use in places where a normal ladder wouldn't work—stairs, corners, uneven terrain, etc. It's great when I need to get the cobwebs out of the skylight over our stairway. I can put two legs on the bottom step and one on the next, and extend my body into the air without fear of disaster.

There's something about "threes." The Godhead is made up of three persons: Father, Son, and Holy Spirit. Man is a combination of three different elements: spirit, soul, and body. Even preachers tend to give three-point sermons! In the life of Jesus, we find three things that helped Him fulfill His mission.

Jesus Knew Where He'd Come From

No one in history had a clearer understanding of where He was from than the Lord Jesus Christ. More than 25 times in the gospels, Jesus explained where He was from. Here are a few examples:

> Anyone who does not honor the Son does not honor the Father who *sent* him....I try to please the One who *sent* me....Whoever hears what I say and believes in the One who *sent* me has eternal life....The things I do, which are the things my Father gave me to do, prove that the Father *sent* me (John 5:23,30,24,36, italics mine).

When Jesus referred to the fact that the Father sent Him, it gave authority to His message. He said, "No one has seen the Father except the One who is from God; only he has seen the Father" (John 6:46).

When Jesus stood before a questioning Pontius Pilate, there was no need for ambivalence before this human ruler, because He knew where He was from.

> Jesus answered, "My kingdom does not belong to this world. If it belonged to this world, my servants would fight so that I would not be given over to the Jews. But my kingdom *is from another place*" (John 18:36, italics mine).

With you and me, it is helpful to have an understanding of our heritage or family history. This is why the subject of "roots" has been popular for so many years.

Years ago, I came to understand my calling better when I studied my family roots. My German heritage contained John Hus, the Bohemian Brethren, Martin Luther, and the Moravians. My Swedish grandfather declared that God spoke to him in an audible voice, telling him to come to the States.

Our lives don't begin out of nowhere. We enter this world created and sent by God, linked to families and cultures that contribute to the people we are today.

Jesus Knew Why He Was Here

Never was a person as secure in knowing why He had been born as Jesus. As a child, His Heavenly Father showed Him what His brief life's work was to be. For years in the carpentry shop, He must have prayed over the detailed aspects of His destiny. He waited with great patience and submission. Then at the right time, He stepped onto the pages of history *to be who He was born to be.*

Early in the gospel of John, Jesus declared:

Just as Moses lifted up the snake in the desert, the Son of Man must also be lifted up. So that everyone who believes can have eternal life in him.

God loved the world so much that he gave his one and only Son so that whoever believes in him may not be lost, but have eternal life. God did not send his Son into the world to judge the world guilty, but to save the world through him....They are judged by this fact: The Light has come into the world (John 3:14-19).

Notice His complete understanding of why He was sent (to reveal God's love for the world), how He was to die (lifted up on a cross), what His death would bring (eternal life to those who believed), and what His mission was (to be the Light from God).

What clarity of purpose! No wonder people left everything behind to follow Him.

In Jesus' encounter with the Samaritan woman in the fourth chapter of John, He openly states that He is the Messiah from God. "Then Jesus said, 'I am he—I, the one talking to you.'"

Later on in what Charles Spurgeon called the golden verse of the Bible, He shares with the woman how *the fulfilling of his life's destiny is that which nourishes him, just as food does the human body:* "My food is to do what the One who sent me wants me to do and to finish his work" (John 4:34).

Jesus lived off the energy that came from fulfilling His life's calling. It was His food. It strengthened and satisfied Him. If it were important for Jesus, just think how necessary it is for us.

Probably the greatest understatement ever made was uttered by Pontius Pilate in John 18:37 when he said to the Lord Jesus, "So you are a king!"

If his eyes had been opened to see, he would have realized that the Maker of heaven and earth, the King of kings and Lord of lords, was standing humbly before him. Jesus then delivered to him the statement of destiny for the ages: "This is *why I was born* and came into the world: *to tell people the truth*" (John 18:37, italics mine).

Jesus Knew Where He Was Going

The final anchor of Jesus' incredible life and ministry was the certainty of knowing His future. This was "the joy set before Him" that helped Him face His deepest valleys and most painful crises. *He knew where He was going.*

When He called Nathaniel to be His disciple, He gave him a glimpse of that future when He said, "You will all see heaven open and 'angels of God going up and coming down' on the Son of Man" (John 1:51). As He neared the end of His life, He began to prepare His followers for the fact that He was leaving and going back to the Father (see John 16:10). In John 16:28, He stated it plainly, "I came from the Father into the world. Now I am leaving the world and going back to the Father."

When you know the certainty of the future, it's easier to live with the pressures of the present. The day Dietrich Bonhoeffer was executed in Nazi Germany, he led a service for his fellow prisoners. Then he walked toward his executioners with joy. He knew he was going to receive his heavenly reward.

Christians have a great advantage over others regarding the certainty of future hope. The end of life's calling marks the beginning of eternity with Christ. Crowns and thrones await us.

I recently prayed with a friend who was in the final days of her life. She was ready to see Jesus, her mother, her husband, and friends who had gone before her. She had finished her course. She faced the future with boldness, though she would have to pass through the shadowy veil of death.

A Complete Sense of Destiny

John 17 is one of my favorite chapters in the New Testament. It contains the prayer that Jesus offered to the Father before His death and resurrection.

In the third through fifth verses, we find the most complete expression of an accomplished life purpose ever recorded. Near the end of His life, Jesus—the Man of Destiny—uttered these words:

> And this is eternal life: that people know you, the only true God, and that they know Jesus Christ, the One you sent. Having finished the work you gave me to do, I brought you glory on earth. And now, Father, give me glory with you; give me the glory I had with you before the world was made.

Notice the three key elements of destiny that are found in this, Jesus' greatest and longest prayer:

- I finished the work you gave me to do—the *present*

- And now, Father, give me glory with

you—the *future*

- Give me the glory I had with you before the world was made—the *past*

In the words of William MacDonald:

Jesus' settled concept of his own identity and of the one who sent him made his leadership rise above popularity. Therefore, he was psychologically impervious to popular praise of himself—it did not inflate him—and to negative criticism of himself—it did not deflate him. Knowing at all times what the Father thought of him gave great evenness and steadiness to his leadership.

Follow Me

Jesus said to His disciples, "Follow me." To obey this command, let's summarize what we've learned about Him:

- Jesus knew where He was from. We can know, also.

- Jesus knew why He was born. God has a plan for us, too.

- Jesus knew where He was going. Our future is equally certain in heaven—after our "job" is done.

- Jesus was launched into His calling through the guidance and inspiration of His Father. Following the lead of our earthly and Heavenly fathers is essential to our own success.

(More on the role of our earthly fathers will be explored in Chapter 16.)

We can be encouraged that Jesus doesn't leave us to work this all out on our own. Rather, the power for success comes from the fact that, as Paul the apostle said:

I do not live anymore—it is Christ who lives in me. I still live in my body, but I live by faith in the Son of God who loved me and gave himself to save me (Galatians 2:20).

We can't do it on our own. But with Jesus in our lives, may we also be able to confidently say someday,

I finished the work You gave me to do. I brought You glory on earth.

For Thought, Discussion, and Action

1. Why did Jesus wait until He was 30 years old to begin His earthly ministry? What was He developing during that time? What can we learn from His example?

2. What are the three "pillars" of a successful life? Which of these are strong in your own life? Which are weak?

3. Discuss with others what made Jesus' life the greatest fulfillment of destiny the world has ever seen. What can you do today to follow His example?

4. Research your family roots to get a better handle on your "past." Obey God in the present. Expectantly wait for and hasten the future coming of Christ's perfect Kingdom.

15

Stop Signs

It was 10:15 a.m., and I had just 15 minutes to get back to church. I gunned my in-laws' car, racing out of the parking lot toward their home, where Shirley and the children were waiting for me. I had promised to pick them up for the second service. If I hurried, I could make it.

We were visiting the Pacific Northwest, and I was guest speaker at the church Shirley's parents attended. The first service finished later than I expected (must have been a long-winded preacher), and now I was under pressure to get back on time.

As I turned down Port Orchard Boulevard a mile from their home, my heart sank. A flashing red light appeared in my rear view mirror.

I pulled off the road, slumped in my seat, and waited for the state patrolman to stroll up to my window.

"Did you know you were doing 45 in a 25-mile-an-hour zone?" he asked. "What's the big hurry?"

I swallowed my pride and confessed. "I'm on my way to pick up my family for church. I'm the preacher."

His eyes widened in disbelief. I squirmed as he looked me over.

Finally, he said, "If you're a preacher, then tell me where in the Bible it says that I have the authority to do what I'm doing."

My mind went blank. His question caught me so off guard that I couldn't remember a thing.

Just then, an inner voice said, *Romans 13.*

"Romans 13?" I stammered.

"That's right!" he said, breaking into a grin. "I'll let you go. But watch your speed."

As he walked back to his patrol car, I thought about the irony. I'd just broken the law to be on time to speak for God.

Destiny Stoppers

All of us get "stopped" at some point while trying to find God's will for our lives. There are many detours and directions we can take, and some people become permanently stalled at a stop sign.

Arthur Miller and Ralph Mattson point out in their excellent books *The Truth about You* and *Finding a Job You Can Love* that 50 to 80 percent of Americans are in the wrong jobs—far removed from what God created them to do. Here's how bad it is:

> Most people wish they could do something other than what they *are* doing....There are thousands of young people who are accused of not having direction in their lives, and most of them want direction but do not know how to find it. There are tens of thousands of adults who want some sense of purpose in their workaday lives, but who have little knowledge of how to go about getting it. There are hundreds of thousands of people who spend their lives as if they were adrift—trapped in their circumstances. There are millions of housewives, students, salesmen, bosses, waitresses, executives, ministers, and auto mechanics who do not fit the lives they lead.
>
> Most people are uncertain about the rightness and usefulness of their lives. They are

looking for signposts that will give them purpose and direction.

Why is there so much apathy, discouragement, and depression in our day and age? The Bible says that there are "stop signs" that can prevent us from finding God's will for our life.

Stop Signs of Self

The greatest hindrances do not come from without, but from within. Someone once said, "We have met the enemy and it is us."

The Bible is clear that the number one thing that separates us from meaning and purpose is sin.

> It is your evil that has separated you from your God. Your sins cause him to turn away from you...Anyone who lives as they live will never have peace (Isaiah 59:2,8).

When we choose to take ourselves away from obedience and relationship to God, we reap the consequences of spiritual darkness. We lose our vision. The lights go out. God is the light.

Let's look at three primary sins that, if allowed to go unchecked, will put a stop sign directly in our way. Each of them is graphically illustrated in the Bible.

The Sin of Pride

As far as we know, the first sin ever committed, and one that cost its perpetrator his eternal destiny, was the sin of pride.

Lucifer, one of the greatest of the angels, lost his position as "the anointed cherub who covers" through pride. Ezekiel 28:17 prophetically records for us his fall: "You became too proud because of your beauty. You ruined your wisdom because of your greatness. I threw you down to the ground."

Isaiah 14:13-15 tells us what Lucifer, or Satan's, problem was: The big "I." "I will go up to heaven. I will put my throne above God's stars. I will sit on the mountain...I will go up above...I will be like God."

Pride always places a barrier in the way to fulfilling our destiny. We must accept who we are (humility) and not try to be what we're not (pride). God is opposed to the proud, but gives grace to the humble (see I Peter 5:5).

The Sin of Unbelief

The tragic life of Judas Iscariot is a sobering illustration of how the sin of unbelief can destroy a person. Judas had been carefully chosen by Jesus to be one of the privileged twelve disciples. Jesus' intention was that ultimately, the Twelve would "sit on twelve thrones, judging the twelve tribes of Israel" (Matthew 19:28). Notice, He says twelve, not eleven. Judas was headed for an incredible destiny.

But somewhere along the line, the sin of unbelief crept into his life. It festered and grew until he became a betrayer. The consequences of his unbelief were suicide and damnation.

Regarding the children of Israel entering the Promised Land, the letter to the Hebrews stated, "They were not allowed to enter and have God's rest, because they did not believe" (Hebrews 3:19).

All of us must believe that the Lord has work for us here, and a future with Him in heaven.

The Sin of Disobedience

He came so close to greatness, and in an instant, lost it all. Saul was chosen by God to be the first king of Israel. He was apparently a godly man with many virtues, besides being head-and-shoulders taller than anyone in Israel. But as he began to fulfill God's will for his life, he crashed into the stop sign of willful disobedience. Let's read God's pathetic words to him:

You acted foolishly! You *haven't obeyed* the command of the Lord your God. If you had obeyed him, the Lord would have made your kingdom continue in Israel always, but now your kingdom will not continue. The Lord has looked for the kind of man he wants. He has appointed him to rule his people, because you *haven't obeyed His command* (I Samuel 13:13,14, italics mine).

Saul could have had an eternal lineage of kingship. But because he disobeyed, that honor was given to David. And every year after his disobedience, Saul's life became darker and more tormented. In the blackness of a destiny lost, he even consulted a witch for guidance. The next day, he was dead.

When we detour off the road of God's plan, we run into a maze of stop signs. Obedience is the key to turning around. Obedience brings us back onto the road, and heads us in the right direction.

These three sins, and the manifestations of them, are the main reasons people don't finish their race victoriously. But there are still some other stop signs that we are likely to encounter.

Stop Signs of God's Testing and Timing

Sin is not the only thing that delays us. There's also the testing and timing of God. One of these is what is termed "death of a vision." Many of us have experienced the devastation of thinking we've heard God's direction, then having everything fall through. It seems the vision has died. We may not understand what God is doing at the time.

Just as metal is heated and bent, molded into its final shape, and tested for strength and durability, so God directs the processing of our lives. God Himself puts stop signs in our lives at various points.

The problem may not be sin in the life of an individual. Rather, God may need time to work on the overall character necessary for that person to achieve his calling. Things are done according to His timetable, not ours.

Let's look at people in the Bible who ran into God's stop signs.

Moses. It took God 40 years to build into His servant the character necessary to deliver the Jewish people. Moses thought he was ready to start his mission at the age of 40, while still in the Egyptian palace. Through the sin of presumption, he launched the deliverance (killing a man), and ended up running into God's stop sign. It forced him to hide in the desert of Midian for 40 more years. Now that's a test.

During that time, Moses learned to humble himself, and grew in character. Then God took down His stop sign, and turned on the green light for Moses to deliver the Israelites from slavery.

Joseph. Psalm 105:17-19 tells of the stop sign God put before Jacob's favorite son: "He sent a man before them, Joseph, who was sold as a slave. They afflicted his feet with fetters, He himself was laid in irons; Until the time that his word came to pass, The word of the Lord *tested him*" (NASB, italics mine).

Notice the sovereignty of God at work in Joseph's life. *God* sent him into slavery. *God* put him in prison for two years. (Can you imagine how Joseph must have questioned his dreams at that point?) This was a time of pruning and purging in Joseph's life. It was a true death of a vision. But after the test was over, in God's perfect timing and way, Joseph came out of his own personal hell to fulfill every bit of his life's calling as ruler over Egypt.

David. How could David have doubted his destiny of being king of Israel? He'd felt the oil poured on his head, and had heard the words of the prophet Samuel on the day of his commissioning.

But years later, he arrived at a God-ordained stop sign where he said to himself, "Now I will perish one day by the hand of Saul." Tired of running, tired of living in caves with fugitives, tired of life, he left the country in despair. For 16 painful months, he lived in exile, dead in destiny, but being prepared in character (see I Samuel 27:1-7).

God's call on his life was clear. But David needed to be molded through God's testing to become the "man after His heart." God pulled him through. Right on divine time.

Every great individual in the Bible was prepared for his life's work through some type of testing. There are no exceptions. Abraham, Isaac, Jacob, Job, Esther, Deborah, Noah, and Elijah all encountered God's stop signs in their lives.

It's the same for us. We will be prepared for our life's work by trials, delays, and purification: God's way of protecting and perfecting our destinies.

Lessons in the Dark

A few years ago, I went through a time of great soul-searching and darkness. Prior to this, the understanding of God's destiny for my life had been opening up like a flower in the springtime. God seemed to bless all that I did and touched.

Then suddenly, it changed. Everything I'd based my future on came crashing down. Months of complete spiritual blackness followed.

Where are you, God? I agonized in my heart. The days dragged by; the silence was deafening. One evening, during this "dark night of the soul," I found myself on a lonely, deserted beach. To my horror, the thought of taking my life crossed my mind.

Although I could not see it then, some of the greatest lessons of my life were learned during this season. They included:

Learning the difference between selfish ambition and personal destiny. God does have a plan for our lives. *Why* we are doing what we're doing becomes the crucial question. Is it for God, or is it for personal glory and self-interest? God wants us to fulfill our design for the right reasons.

Learning to wait. How impatient we are! We want God's will, and we want it now (whether it's God's time or not). But God is not in a hurry. That's why Romans 5:3,4 says that we can "also have joy with our troubles, because we know that these troubles produce patience. And patience produces character, and character produces hope."

Learning to love God for who He is. We should not love Him merely because of our circumstances or what He does for us. God does not owe us anything. Times of testing remind us that God is worthy of our lives, our love, and our praise, regardless of what happens to us.

Learning to cry in brokenness before Him. We are dependent upon God, and need to be assured that "God will not reject a heart that is broken and sorry for sin" (Psalm 51:17). Success tends to harden us. Testing and delay are used by God to keep our hearts humble and usable.

Learning true faith, which is primarily forged through affliction. When darkness comes, we want to hold Daddy's hand, and cling to him for protection. When we can "see," we often run ahead on our own, and get into trouble. Testing strengthens our childlike faith. It brings us back to reality, which is our desperate need to cling to God.

Learning to die. "Dying," in the spiritual sense, means that we must be willing to lay aside our desires, our manipulations, our ambitions, and our carnal desires. Out of death comes the sweetness of life with Christ. "It is no longer I that live, but Christ that lives in me." God's testing in our lives is an act of crucifixion that leads to resurrection power in our spirits and ministries.

I'm Stopped!

Many of you may feel that you are at a stop sign in your spiritual life. Your delay may be due to pride, unbelief, disobedience, or selfish choices that have separated you from God. Or you may be in a season of testing to prepare you for the future.

If sin is causing your holdup, it's time to repent and move forward. You've stopped yourself. Only by removing the obstacle you put there can you get back on pathway that your Heavenly Father has laid out for you.

Once you return, you will still encounter His testing and timing that are necessary for success. Accept His loving disciplines in your life, and press through the darkness with humility and courage. On the other side, the sun will be shining more brightly than ever before.

For Thought, Discussion, and Action

1. What is the primary thing that stops people from finding God's will for their lives? In what different forms does this stop sign reveal itself?

2. Why does God produce some stop signs in the pathway of our destiny? Can you think of any He has placed in your life? Why did He do it?

3. When God allows us to go through a "death of a vision," what kinds of lessons is He trying to teach us? Can you name all six? Have you ever faced any of these in your own life? Share.

4. Determine what stop signs are currently in your own life. Remove the ones that are sin. Wait on God for His way and timing for the release of your own personal destiny.

16

Ask and It Shall Be Given

It's amazing how little things take on such importance. Ocean liners are towed by small boats. Sophisticated computers are useless without tiny microchips. A smile or kind word can make all the difference in the world in human relationships.

In this chapter, we will look at a simple little key to discovering your destiny. Jesus talked about it in His Sermon on the Mount when He said:

Ask, and God will give to you. *Search,* and you will find. *Knock,* and the door will open for you. Yes, everyone who asks will receive. Everyone who searches will find. And everyone who knocks will have the door opened.

If your children *ask* for bread, which of you would give them a stone? Or if your children *ask* for a fish, would you give them a snake? Even though you are bad, you know how to give good gifts to your children. How much more your heavenly Father will give good things to those who *ask Him!* (Matthew 7:7-11, italics mine).

Glad You Asked

God is the source of all knowledge and power, and we are totally dependent on Him to guide and sustain us. The bridge that God has erected between His sufficiency and our need is our commitment to *humbly seek Him.*

The key to knowing what God has planned for our life is to *ask*. (You didn't *ask* until now, so I didn't tell you!)

And notice what Jesus says about the way we are to ask: We are to *continue* asking, *continue* searching, *continue* knocking, *until* the answer comes. In the Greek language, these words are in the *aorist* tense, which is the present continuous mode. We are to "keep on keeping on" until we receive God's answer.

The God of the universe has promised that He will faithfully answer every sincere, persistent request. But God doesn't like casual or nonpersistent followers. We can't seek Him halfheartedly.

When I was 19 years old and on the verge of making the most important vocational decisions of my life, the Lord led me to set aside a day to fast and seek Him. (I had been praying for over a year regarding His will for my life.) Early one morning, I went to a favorite secluded beach and began to pray. I lifted up my options before the Lord. I read Scripture for hours, and determined that I would not go home until God had spoken to me.

After nearly eight hours, I felt led to turn to one particular Scripture. Then another and another. They all contained precise confirmations that I was to go to Europe for missions training. A month later, I left for Germany.

For 20 years now, I have served in missions. How glad I am that God clearly guided me. How glad He was that I asked.

Ask Your Earthly Father

One of the first ways that God reveals His plans for our lives is through the counsel and guidance of our earthly fathers. This may seem like a strange concept to some, but it is clearly taught in the Bible, and is confirmed in the life stories of many respected people. Your human father plays a significant role in the formation of your character. One of the greatest problems for many young people today is the literal or spiritual absence of dads in their lives.

The Bible says, "The glory of children is their father" (Proverbs 17:6 NKJV). Whereas mothers primarily model God's attributes of love and tenderness, a child will look to his father for authoritative direction in life. The primary role of a father is to impart a sense of destiny.

My favorite example of this is Zechariah, father of John the Baptist. After recovering from his unbelief, and following the birth of his son John, he prophesied in Luke 1:76-79 regarding the lifework of his baby son:

> Now you, child, will be called a prophet of the Most High God. You will go before the Lord to prepare his way. You will make his people know that they will be saved by having their sins forgiven. With the loving mercy of our God, a new day from heaven will dawn upon us. It will shine on those who live in darkness, in the shadow of death. It will guide us into the path of peace.

Can you imagine how many times Zechariah reminded John of the circumstances of his birth and his destiny throughout his growing-up years? You can almost hear Zechariah say, "John, an angel told us your name, and that your purpose in life was to prepare the way for God's Messiah. You are to be a prophet to prepare Israel for God's coming. God showed me so. Remember these things, young John. Pray over them. God has a plan for you."

That's the role of a father: to point the way. To help his children discover their gifts and callings. To become coach and head cheerleader.

It's well known that one of the great strengths of the traditional Jewish home is the role that the father plays in guiding his children into their future vocations. Is this why Jewish sons have a reputation for doing so well in the business world? Have Jewish dads simply modeled a biblical idea?

When I pray over my own five children at bedtime each night, God reminds me of the incredible influence I have to either dash their dreams or help them blossom. They look to me more than any other person on earth for their life direction.

For those of you who have no fathers, or who have a poor relationship to your dad, God will serve as your Father, and He will provide other father figures for you. Jesus lost Joseph, and His Heavenly Father filled the void. King Josiah had an evil father, but God provided mentors to guide him to become a righteous king.

Whether it's through your own dad or through a substitute that God provides, your Heavenly Father will give you direction. Love the person that He brings into your life. Listen to him. Live in the shelter of his counsel.

Ask Others

Though God is the one who most perfectly understands our purpose, He chooses many means to share that revelation with us. He gives us parents. He speaks through His word, the Bible. He sends His Spirit to live inside us and guide us. But He also dwells in other godly people—relatives, friends, pastors, and mentors—whom He places in our lives.

Loren Cunningham, founder of Youth With A Mission, says that *the humbler we are, the more authorities we will recognize in our lives.* Proverbs 15:22 tells us, "Plans fail without good advice, but they succeed with the advice of many others."

Our own insecurities make it difficult for us to view ourselves objectively. We may have the gift of encouragement, but because of low self-esteem due to a troubled childhood or a broken relationship, we may have convinced ourselves that we have nothing to offer others. We may possess a musical talent, but because of shyness, we may fail to develop it the way God intended. Friends and spiritual leaders can help us overcome our blind spots.

After killing and imprisoning Christians, Paul probably had a pretty low view of how God could use him in ministry. Then Barnabas entered his life and through his gift of encouragement and counsel, Barnabas convinced Paul that God had a call on his life. (Ananias was the first "friend" God used to confirm Paul's life purpose to him. See Acts 9:10-19.)

None of us are meant to find our way alone. Whether we realize it or not, God has already placed people around us who have spiritual insight into our gifts, aptitudes, and calling. These people might be a pastor or youth leader, close friend, spiritual mentor, fellow worker or peer, or someone else God will bring your way.

In my life, God has especially used visiting evangelists, Bible teachers, and spiritual leaders who have prayed for me (oftentimes with the laying on of hands, similar to Paul's ministry to Timothy in II Timothy 1:6) to impart gifts and words of understanding regarding God's purpose for me.

Seek their counsel. Ask them if God has revealed to them anything regarding your calling or future. Ask what suggestions they have for your spiritual development. Ask them to point out your strengths and weaknesses. The more advice you get, the better. The Scripture says, "You need advice when you go to war. If you have lots of good advice, you will win" (Proverbs 24:6).

There are also specific ministries that God has raised up to help guide us. One that has blessed my life, Lifework Consulting Services, uses the SIMA (System for Identifying Motivated Abilities) process to help people understand how God has designed them and what types of jobs would be best for them. In Youth With A Mission (and many other Christian organizations), the SIMA process is used to help place people in the best possible position for using their God-given gifts.

If you're interested in the SIMA process, please contact: Lifework Consulting Services, 303 W. Dravus Street, Seattle, WA 98119, Tel: (206) 284-5442.

Ask Your Heavenly Father

While I was studying in New Zealand a number of years ago, a spiritual leader named Blythe Harper spoke to me regarding future ministry. While addressing a room full of young people and their families, he spoke of the future. He then looked directly into my eyes and quoted Jeremiah 29:11-14:

> "I say this because I know what I am planning for you," says the Lord. "I have good plans for you, not plans to hurt you. I will give you hope and a good future. Then you will call my name. You will come to me and pray to me, and I will listen to you. You will search for me. And when you search for me with all your heart, you will find me! I will let you find me," says the Lord.

When he spoke those words, it felt like an arrow had pierced my heart. The God of the universe wanted to tell me His plans for my life. How could I reach Him? By searching for Him with all my heart. If I did, He promised (on His infinite word of honor) that: "I will let you find me."

From that day on, I began to *ask the one who knows it all.* As I have sought Him with a whole heart, He has been faithful to make His plans known to me. It has not always been easy nor clear. But by seeking God I have found Him, and in Him, my destiny.

Paul said of us all:

> God began by making one person, and

from him came all the different people who live everywhere in the world. God decided exactly when and where they must live. God wanted them to *look for him* and perhaps *search all around for him and find him,* though he is not far from any of us: "We live in him. We walk in him. We are in him" (Acts 17:26-28, italics mine).

We have arrived at the simple bottom line of learning your destiny: *seek your Heavenly Father with all your heart until you find Him.* We are not talking here about casual, curious petitions. God is worthy of much more than that. The price of revelation is the cost of developing an intimate relationship.

From this we also learn what is one of man's greatest sins: the sin of *prayerlessness.* When so many people lack direction in their lives, they must have neglected to seek God in prayer. Paul said, "He is not far from any of us." He's as close as a sincere, persistent, wholehearted prayer.

How about You?

Ross Tooley was a young New Zealander with a sense of God's call on his life. One evening, after hearing a message on the importance of seeking God's will for his life, young Ross locked himself in his room and determined to seek the Lord.

Laying out a map of the world on the floor, he cried out to God, "Lord, I am not leaving this room until You speak to me. I want to do Your will. Where do You want me to go? What do You want me to do?"

By morning, he had his message and his destiny. Many fruitful years of ministry were to come out of that one desperate night of seeking God's face.

Why don't you begin right now to discover the joy of unlocking God's will for your life by listening to your earthly father, seeking the counsel of those God has placed around you, and, especially, developing an intimate and personal relationship with your Heavenly Father.

As Jeremiah said:

"Thus says the Lord who made the earth, the Lord who formed it to establish it, the Lord is His name, 'Call to Me, and I will answer you, and I will tell you great and mighty things, which you do not know'" (Jeremiah 33:2,3 NASB).

Great and mighty things are yours for the asking.

For Thought, Discussion, and Action

1. Why did God design our relationship with Him to function around the principle of asking? Why does He sometimes make us persevere in seeking Him?

2. Name the three primary sources of guidance that we have in life. Which of these have you used effectively? Which have you neglected?

3. Share a situation in which God used your father or a friend to help give direction to your life. Did you realize at the time that God was really speaking through them?

4. Set aside a time to really seek God about your future. Keep seeking Him for the rest of your life.

17

I Think I Messed Up!

Have you ever wondered what happens when you stray off the pathway of God's plan for your life? It's easy to mess up.

Simon Peter had that experience. Hurry and find your seat. The curtain is rising on Scene Two of his life. You may find some encouragement here from a man many of us can identify with.

Peter's Destiny—Scene Two

Under cover of a hazy moonlight, an angry crowd approached the garden. Their torches and lanterns were the only things that signaled their approach. They were carrying weapons.

Peter gasped at the sight. *There's Judas!* he thought. *Judas is leading the high priest and a group of soldiers!* Rousing himself from the spot where he, James, and John had fallen asleep, Peter bolted to his feet and turned to face the mob.

Jesus had admonished him about falling asleep and not praying. His Lord looked drained, yet determined. They'd been to the Garden of Gethsemane many times before, but nothing like this had ever happened. Peter trembled.

"Master," Judas broke the silence with brazen hypocrisy, yet timidity in his voice. Drawing close to Jesus, he greeted Him with the traditional Hebrew kiss, though never looking Him in the eye. Jesus answered him back with anguish and concern in His voice. Peter couldn't quite hear the words, but he knew something was wrong. Terribly wrong.

They're going to arrest Him! Peter suddenly realized. Adrenalin rushed through his body. *James, John, and I are the only ones who can save Him.* Guards stepped forward to bind the arms of Jesus. Peter drew his sword to protect his Lord and friend.

Peter's sword connected with human flesh, sending one of the men writhing to the ground with a blood-curdling scream. A small object lay near him, staining the ground crimson.

The man looked up at Peter in horror. Standing next to him was his master, the Jewish high priest, the number one holy man of Israel. Peter's stomach twisted into knots. He had just cut off the right ear of the high priest's servant!

Somewhere deep inside, Peter knew that he had messed up. Maybe enough to cost him his destiny.

Setting the Stage

I remember the first time I meditated on this story found in Luke 22:47-53 and John 18:1-14. What an incredible night that must have been in the Garden of Gethsemane. Jesus was approaching the fulfillment of His mission. To strengthen Himself for the final test, He'd retreated with His closest followers to a favorite place of prayer. There He'd knelt three times and poured out His heart to God. His disciples had been too tired and unaware to join Him in this crucial hour.

After gently rebuking Peter, James, and John for failing to keep watch with Him, Jesus was confronted by Judas leading the temple guards to arrest Him. In the bedlam that followed, only one act of violence is mentioned: in impulsive rage and protectiveness, Peter drew his sword and cut off the ear of the high priest's slave. Luke only mentions the ear severing. John tells who did it.

To understand the significance of Peter's blunder and how it could have cost him the fulfillment of his life purpose, we need to turn back to an earlier scene in Peter's life. After calling him to become a "fisher of men," Jesus had clearly revealed to Peter the destiny that God had for him. It took place near a town named Caesarea Philippi.

Peter's Destiny—Scene One

What a week! Healings every day. Four thousand people fed from seven loaves and a few fish. Peter was sure that Jesus was no ordinary man. *And Jesus has chosen me to be one of His close followers!* he thought to himself as the Twelve walked with the Lord along the dusty road to Caesarea Philippi.

Will He establish His Kingdom soon? the young apostle wondered. *What role will I play in this glorious new age?*

Coming to a grove of olive trees shading a well-used rest area for travelers, Jesus told His disciples to stop for a moment to refresh themselves. As they sat on the ground, Jesus surprised them with a question that only one was prepared to answer.

"Who do you say I am?" asked the Master. Peter rose with the confidence of one who knew.

"You are the Christ, the Son of the living God." He spoke with great conviction, then sat down. Every eye was now focused on Jesus. They all awaited confirmation.

Jesus didn't answer them directly. (He rarely answered them directly.) Looking down the corridor of time, with pride and certain pronouncement, He looked into Peter's eyes and imparted to him a sense of destiny:

You are blessed, Simon son of Jonah, because no person taught you that. My Father in heaven showed you who I am. So I tell you, you are Peter. On this rock I will build my church, and the power of death will not be able to defeat it. I will give you the keys of the kingdom of heaven; the things you don't allow on earth will be the things that God does not allow, and the things you allow on earth will be the things that God allows (Matthew 16:17-19).

Peter sat dumbfounded. Jesus had just given him a new name. Didn't that happen only when God was about to use an individual in an unusual way? His heart was racing. And what was that about building a church around him and giving him keys to the kingdom of heaven?

Jesus put His arm around Peter as the group headed back down the road. He loved this rough, tough fisherman. The Father had shown the Son that this boisterous, impetuous man—Simon Peter, the fisherman—was destined to be the leader of the disciples and the early church. But He also knew that fulfilling God's plan for his life wouldn't be easy. He would need some help along the way.

That brings us back to Scene Two in the Garden of Gethsemane. Peter, the "rock" upon which the early church was to be built, had committed not just an impetuous act, but a crime:

- He had assaulted a person with a deadly weapon.
- The evidence was clear—the ear had been cut off.
- The victim wasn't just any person. He was the slave of the main legal and religious leader of the nation, the High Priest.
- Peter would certainly go to prison. He had messed up big time.

Join the Club

Peter's story is not unique. The Bible says that we "all have sinned and are not good enough for God's glory" (Romans 3:23). All of us have deviated in some way from God's perfect pathway for our lives. We've made choices that were not His will. We've plunged into sin for days, months, or even years. Like Jonah, some of us have even run away from His plans for our lives.

None of us except Jesus has lived a perfect life. Somewhere along the line, *each of us has messed up.*

Fortunately, our loving Father does not just write us off. We are all dependent on His grace and redeeming love. He is always working redemptively with our choices and mistakes.

For a number of years, I worried about achieving God's "best" for my life. It was good motivation for a Christ-centered life. But my concept of "best" was too rigid. Somewhere inside of me, I'd subconsciously drawn the conclusion that there was only one "best" road for me. If I missed that one, then there were few paths left open to me.

In the Bible, I found that the emphasis was different. Instead of focusing on what had been "lost," God was always creating new possibilities for people. They would break, and He would mend. They would sin, and He would forgive. They would lose, and He would restore. The emphasis was always on God's ability to creatively resurrect their destiny if a person would return to obedience to Him.

The Bible's list of repaired or resurrected destinies is almost endless: Abraham, Jacob, Joseph, Moses, Samson, David, Hezekiah, Elijah, Jeremiah, Daniel, Job, Paul, and yes—Peter. All of them sinned, putting their destiny either in jeopardy or on hold. But God came through to offer them new life and hope, and to propel them forward.

The key was God's grace and willingness to give

them another chance. That brings us back to Simon Peter. God wasn't through with him yet.

Peter's Destiny—Scene Three

Sweat dripped off his brow as Peter looked at the damage he'd inflicted. Blood was streaming down the neck of the high priest's slave. Everyone seemed frozen until Jesus broke the silence. "Peter," He said, "put your sword back. Shouldn't I drink the cup the Father gave me?"

Peter blinked back tears. It seemed that all hope was lost with the arrest of his Master and Lord.

But Jesus stepped forward and put His hand on the slave's bloodied head. When He pulled His hand away, a new ear had replaced the old one.

The crowd gasped. A person's destiny had just been rescued. Peter had been delivered from the consequences of his crime.

Jesus had done it by destroying the evidence.

Our Maker and Remaker

After denying the Lord Jesus and experiencing His crucifixion and resurrection from the dead, Peter went on to fulfill his calling as the leading apostle of the early church. The one who had made him years before was faithful to "remake" him following his impetuous crime and cowardly denial.

Yes, he'd messed up. Yes, he'd done wrong. But God was ready to *make all things new and restore him to the pathway of obedience.* He will always salvage a life put back into His care.

The same is true of us. Some of you may have stepped off the roadway of God's plan for your life. Maybe it was due to:

- abusive and ungodly parents
- the grief and heartache of divorce
- years wasted with alcohol, drugs, or sexual sin

- the committing of a crime
- or years spent in apathy and ignorance

No matter how you've messed up, God specializes in healing and restoration. He doesn't always take away all the consequences of sin. But He longs to show us mercy and remake us into His image.

I have a good friend named Lori. Lori faithfully served God for a number of years. Then she walked away from Him, and for seven years, she struggled with various forms of sin and despair. Hunting for love, hardened by affluence, wounded by divorce, and devastated by the loss of a child, Lori eventually called Shirley and me one evening. She knew she was not living God's destiny for her life. She wanted to get back onto the pathway of His calling.

We cried together over the phone with Lori many times over the next few months. We counseled her and prayed with her.

Lori slowly began to clean out the cobwebs of a disobedient life, and she returned to her first love of Jesus. It didn't happen instantly. But eventually, she allowed the Lord Jesus to repair and restore her. Today Lori is in an exciting counseling ministry.

If you've messed up, be encouraged. "The law came to make sin worse. But when sin grew worse, God's grace increased" (Romans 5:20). Messing up makes us candidates for grace.

He restored Peter. He'll do the same for you and for me.

For Thought, Discussion, and Action

1. In what areas of your life can you relate to Peter? Share an example with others.

2. What do we mean that God has a "creative potential" for your life? Isn't there just one "best" path? Explain.

3. Discuss the lives of people in the Bible who

messed up along the way. How did God get them to return to His pathway of obedience? What can you learn from their example?

4. Aren't you glad that God is committed to picking us up when we fall? Thank Him for saving you! Thank Him for His forgiveness and redeeming power! Promise that you will not abuse His grace.

18

Begin the Adventure

Do you remember your first Easter egg hunt? The thrill of the chase, the joy of being first to fill your basket?

Seeking to fulfill your destiny is like going on a lifelong Easter egg hunt. It's an adventure of discovery. There are lots of directions to go, and lots of distractions to throw you off course. Some searches will come up empty. But the joy of each success will make the memory of failure quickly fade.

Two things are certain: If you don't play the game, you'll miss out on the adventure. But if you do play the game, you will be rewarded.

I hope that by now, you are convinced that God wants you to seek out the destiny that He planned for you.

He wants you to *believe* that you have a destiny:

- to see His plan for your life.

- to reject the lie of evolution, and embrace the beauty of your unique design and calling.

- to set high and worthy goals that can be pursued for a lifetime.

God longs for you to *achieve* your destiny through the development of inner strength and character:

- to anchor your heart in goodness.

- to grow in all aspects of knowledge.

- to order your pursuits through self-control.
- to be patient under pressure and tests.
- to become like Him through prayer and His word.
- to radiate His kindness to others.
- to model the expanse of His love.

And finally, He wants you to *receive* His plans for your life and live them to the fullest by:

- imitating those who have gone before—especially the perfect example of our Lord Jesus Christ.
- to move past the stop signs of sin, testing, and ignorance.
- to ask, and know that you will find.
- to let God pick you up when you fall.

When you live out your calling, you bring glory to God as your Maker, participate in His global plans for salvation, and enjoy a lifetime of meaning and fulfillment.

It doesn't get any better than that!

Yeah, Paul!

That's what the apostle Paul did. He had a rough start. He was even an enemy of God and His truth. But when Jesus spoke to Paul on the road to Damascus, he realized he was going the wrong way. He spun around and marched straight into his God-ordained destiny. This is how he retold the story years later:

Then I heard a voice speaking to me in the Jewish language, saying, "Saul, Saul, why are you persecuting me? *You are only hurting yourself by fighting Me.*" [Notice what happens when we resist God's plans for our lives. We only end up hurting ourselves.] I said, "Who are you, Lord?" The Lord said, "I am Jesus, the one you are persecuting. Stand up! I have chosen you to be my servant and my witness—you will tell people the things that you have seen and the things that I will show you. This is why I have come to you today. I will keep you safe from your own people and also from those who are not Jewish. I am sending you to them to open their eyes so that they may turn away from darkness to the light, away from the power of Satan and to God. Then their sins can be forgiven, and they can have a place with those people who have been made holy by believing in me."

"King Agrippa, after I had this vision from heaven, I obeyed it. I began telling people that they should change their hearts and lives and turn to God...But God has helped me, and so I stand here today, telling all people, small and great, what I have seen" (Acts 26:14-22, italics mine).

Paul had a "D-Day" in his life when he began the adventure of following God. His "D-Day" was his Damascus Day—his Destiny Day. Years later, in a number of his letters, he would refer to the importance of living for his created purpose, and encourage others to do the same.

To his friends in Corinth he wrote:

Each one of us did the work God gave us to do. I planted the seed, and Apollos watered it. But God is the One who made it grow....using the gift God gave me, I laid the foundation (I Corinthians 3:5,6,10, italics mine.)

To the Galatians, he shared that:

God had special plans for me and set me apart for his work even before I was born. He called me through his grace and showed his son to me so that I might tell the Good News about him to those who are not Jewish (Galatians 1:15, italics mine).

The greeting in his letters to both the Ephesian and Colossian Christians was simply this:

> From Paul, an apostle of Christ Jesus. *I am an apostle because that is what God wanted* (Ephesians 1:1 and Colossians 1:1, italics mine).

And to Titus he wrote:

> From Paul, a servant of God and an apostle of Jesus Christ. *I was sent to help the faith of God's chosen people and to help them know the truth that shows people how to serve God* (Titus 1:1, italics mine).

Paul was so convinced of the importance of fulfilling our calling that he encouraged his disciple Timothy with the following destiny-laden words:

> *Use the gift you have,* which was given to you through prophecy when the group of elders laid their hands on you. Continue to do those things; *give your life to doing them* (I Timothy 4:14,15, italics mine).

> This is why I remind you *to keep using the gift God gave you* when I laid my hands on you. Now let it grow, as a small flame grows into a fire (II Timothy 1:6, italics mine).

> In the sight of God, who gives life to everything, and of Christ Jesus, I give you a command....Do what you were commanded to do without wrong or blame until our Lord Jesus Christ comes again (I Timothy 6:13,14).

And to another friend, named Archippus, he asked the Colossian church to pass on the following reminder:

> Tell Archippus, "Be sure to finish the work the Lord gave you" (Colossians 4:17).

Good advice from a very wise man. He lived his life's destiny, and wanted others to do the same.

Destined to Seek and to Serve

When you boil it all down, fulfilling your destiny in life can be summed up by *seeking* first the Kingdom of God and His righteousness, then *serving* in that Kingdom with the gifts and abilities God has given you. We must:

- seek to know the King, who gives each of us a purpose and place in His Kingdom.

- seek His character or righteousness, for without it, we cannot accomplish our God-given tasks.

- seek His vision and perspective for our lives, and learn of our gifts and calling.

- seek to be a servant.

Our destiny is not something that can be accomplished in isolation. It is inseparably connected to the One who created it, and to the only One who can provide the power necessary for its fulfillment.

Many people fail to live their destinies because they are separated from God and His eternal plans. They must begin by being born again into a restored relationship with the Father.

Once we are in God's Kingdom, three things are necessary to make us good, productive servants. First of all, we need to *know our Master*. Second, we need to *know our responsibilities*. No one can serve well if they don't clearly see their assigned task, along with its duties and boundaries.

Third, we need to *perform His responsibilities well for the sake of the Master*. God will provide the tools and inspiration. All He asks is our cooperation. No wonder the writers of the New Testament almost always signed their letters as "servants of Christ." Being a servant of God is the bottom line of human destiny. For more on this subject, see my first book, *Leadership for the 21st Century*.

A Magnificent Obsession

Years ago, a spiritual leader told me that I needed to have a "magnificent obsession" for Christ. It needed to be worth all my time and energy. It needed to be my reason for living.

I was reminded of what I had once heard:

A vision without a task makes a visionary.

A task without a vision is drudgery.

But a vision with a task makes a missionary.

How about you? Do you have a vision and a task? Do you have a magnificent obsession about God and the life He has planned for you?

If not, then *begin the adventure today.*

Paul told King Agrippa, "I did not prove disobedient to the heavenly vision" (Acts 26:19 NASB). Near the end of his life, Paul said confidently, "I have fought the good fight, I have finished the race, I have kept the faith. Now, a crown is being held for me...not only to me but to all those who have waited with love for him to come again" (II Timothy 4:7,8). God wants each of us to wear one of those crowns.

Think about the following statements from Larry Tomczak's book, *Victorious Living at the End of the Age.* Their content is taken almost entirely from the Bible. Make them your statement of commitment today and for the rest of your life:

The eyes of the Lord run to and fro throughout the whole earth in order to show Himself strong in behalf of those whose hearts are fully blameless toward Him. God rewards those who diligently seek Him. He who calls me is faithful and He will do it.

I'm not lukewarm. I'm not a compromiser. I'll not be conformed to this world. I'm not a loser; I'm a winner. I'm a partaker of His divine nature. God indwells my body. I run the race to win. His grace is sufficient for me. His power is made perfect in weakness.

When the enemy comes in like a flood, the
Spirit of the Lord will raise up a standard. I'm
a part of that standard. We are soldiers of the
army of salvation that God is raising up to
save this world. I'll not despise the day of
small beginnings. We will reclaim that which
the thief has stolen through tradition and ignorance. The earth is the Lord's and the full-
ness thereof, the world and all who dwell
therein.

He said He would pour out His Spirit in
these last days. Sons and daughters would
prophesy, young men would see visions, old
men would dream dreams. I'm a part of this
end-time vision, for without it, I will perish.
For still the vision awaits its time, it hastens
to the end, it will not fail. If it seems slow I
will wait for it. It will surely come. It will not
delay. Therefore, *I have a sense of destiny.*

Jesus is restoring His church. He is coming
back for a glorious church without spot or
wrinkle or blemish or any such thing. It will
be a triumphant church. It will kick the gates
of hell in. I'm a part of this end-time move.
I'm a pioneer; I'm not a settler. I'm on the front
lines. I've counted the cost. I'll pay the price.
I'm giving my utmost for His highest. I press
on toward the goal for the prize of the high
call of God in Christ Jesus, my Lord.

I'm out to change my generation. I'm beginning today. I redeem the time. I'm not
weighed down by the cares of this life. I cast
my cares on the Lord. Whatever the task this
day, I'll do it heartily as serving the Lord. I'll
pursue excellence because I serve a God of
excellence. I stir up the gifts within me. I'll
step out in faith. I'll move in the supernatural.
I'll set the captives free.

The Spirit of the Lord is upon me. He has anointed me to preach good news to the poor. He has sent me to proclaim release to the captives, recovery of sight to the blind, to set at liberty those who are oppressed, to bind up the brokenhearted, and to proclaim the acceptable year of the Lord.

I'll not limit the Holy One of Israel. *I'll not be disobedient to the heavenly vision.* The kingdoms of this world shall become the kingdoms of our God and of His Christ!

Now to Him Who is able to keep me from falling and to present me without blemish before the presence of His glory with exceeding joy, to the only God, my Savior, through Jesus Christ my Lord be glory, majesty, dominion, and authority before all time and now and forever! Amen!

Yes, God has a plan for your life. He wants you to begin today to be the person He created you to be. Trust Him. Seek Him. *You have a destiny. Go for it!*

For Thought, Discussion, and Action

1. Why is Paul a good example of a person who fulfilled his destiny? Did he make any mistakes? Did he take any wrong turns? What were some of the keys to his success?

2. How is fulfilling God's plan for your life synonymous with "seeking first His kingdom and His righteousness"?

3. Why is being a servant a good picture of fulfilling God's purpose for our lives? Can you name the three keys to being a good servant?

4. Go for it!

Afterword

As I look back over the years of God's leading in my life, three practical things stand out as major helpers along the way. I pass them on to aid you in your own search:

1. *Read lots of biographies* of great men and women of God. They are inspiring, insightful, down to earth, and show examples of how God both destines and leads His people. You'll pick up ideas that will be beneficial to your own life. You can find them at your local library, Christian bookstore, or by contacting YWAM Publishing (see the following pages).

2. *Attach yourself to a person with a sense of destiny.* Proverbs says, "Spend time with the wise and you will become wise, but the friends of fools will suffer" (Proverbs 13:20). You become like those you hang around with. Want to have a sense of destiny? Spend time with a person who recognizes his. It could be your parent, sibling, friend, youth leader, teacher, or pastor. Pray that God will give you a mentoring relationship with a person who is pursuing God's plan. I guarantee that it will rub off.

3. *Attend a Youth With A Mission Discipleship Training School or another dynamic training program.* A YWAM DTS changed my entire life. It was there that I read many inspiring biographies and was surrounded by people with a sense of destiny, not only for their own lives, but for the cause of world evangelism. Participating in this five-month "spiritual greenhouse" was one of the greatest investments of time and money that I ever made. God used it to help me know Him better and to find my place in His advancing Kingdom on earth.

Youth With A Mission has a global university called the *University of the Nations,* with training centers in over 80 countries. The five-month Discipleship Training School is the introductory course, and can be taken in many nations. If you are interested, please write or call the regional YWAM centers listed below:

The Americas: YWAM DTS, P.O. Box 4600, Tyler, TX 75712, Tel. (903) 882-5591, Fax (903) 882-7673.

Europe, Middle East, Africa: YWAM DTS, 13 Highfield Oval, Ambrose Lane, Harpenden, Herts. AL5 4BX, England, Tel. 011-44-582-7654-81, Fax 011-44-582-7680-48.

YWAM North American Office: P.O. Box 55309, Seattle, WA 98155, Tel. (206) 363-9844, Fax (206) 363-9845.

Pacific and Asia: University of the Nations, 75-5851 Kuakini Hwy., Kailua-Kona, HI 96740, Tel. (808) 326-7228, Fax (808) 329-2387.

If you are under eighteen, you should know about YWAM's international ministry called King's Kids, which helps launch children into their God-given destinies. It's a life-changer! Please contact them at: King's Kids International, P.O. Box 117, Kailua-Kona, HI 96745-0117, Tel. (808) 329-5745.